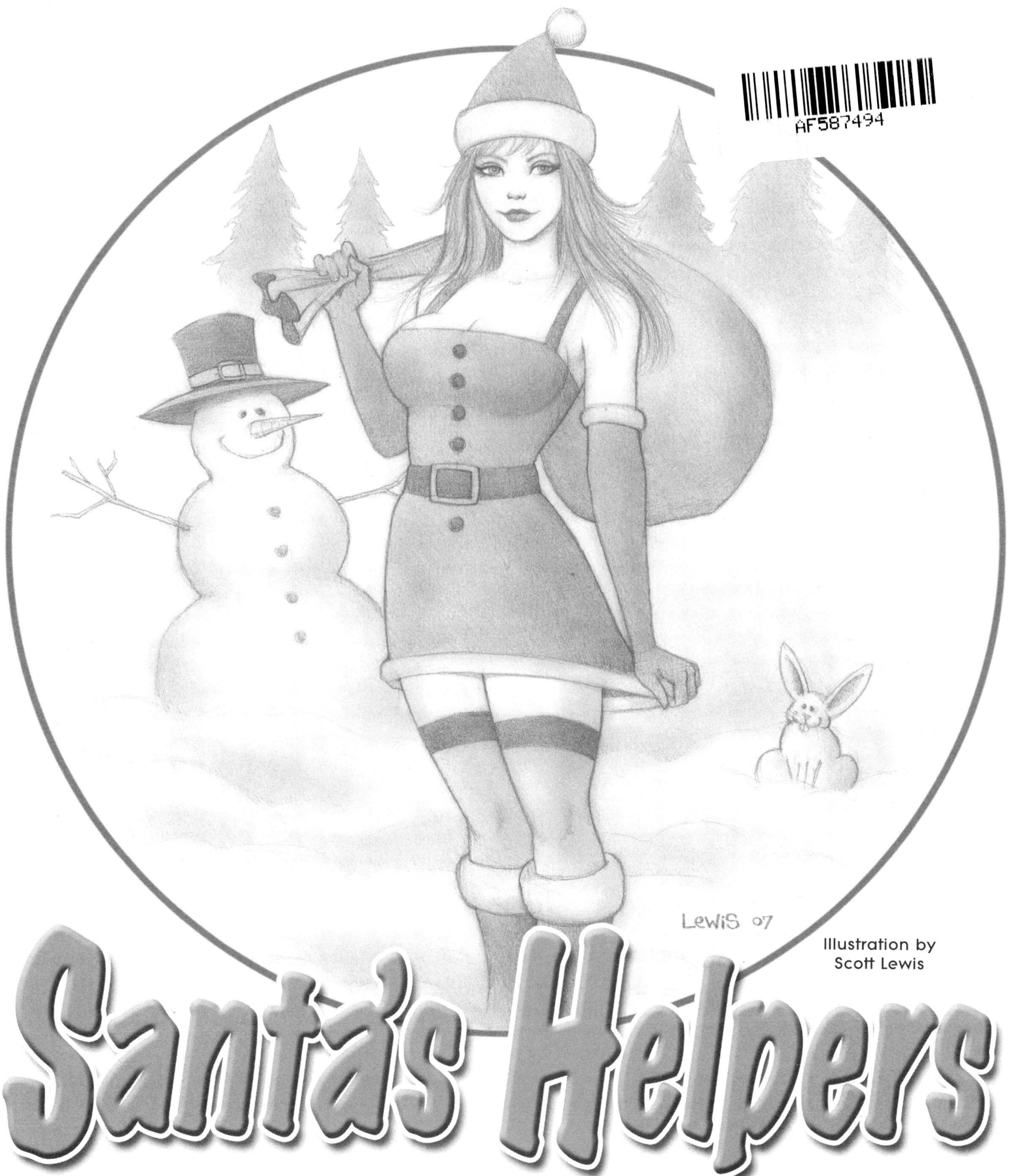

Illustration by
Scott Lewis

Santa's Helpers

Or, how DOES Old St. Nick stay so damned warm & jolly all year 'round? Ho-Ho-Ho indeed!

A GALLERY GIRLS COLLECTION

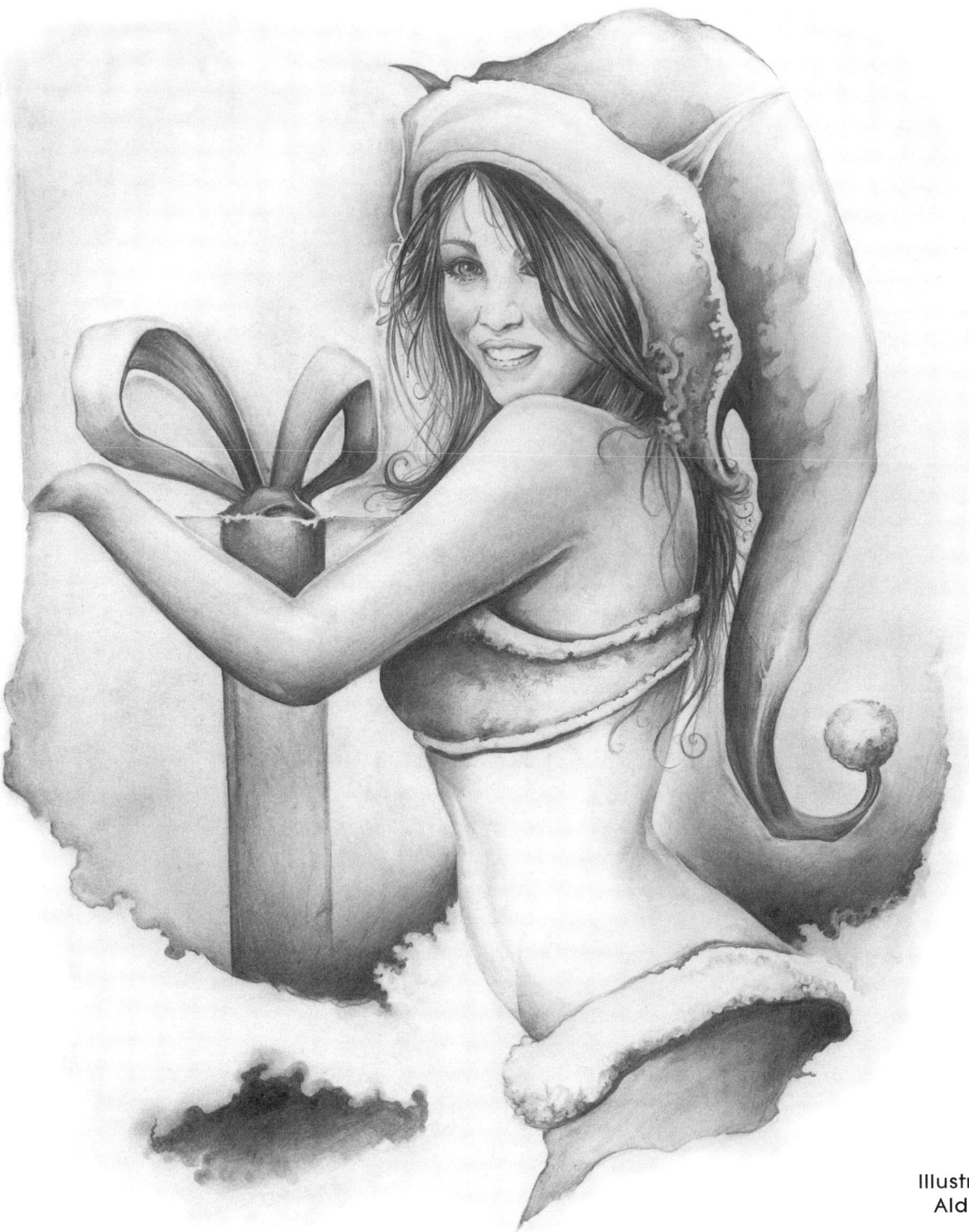

Illustration by
Aldo Perez

SANTA'S HELPERS

Volume One

Book design by Grassy Knoll Studios.

Published by
SQP Inc.
PO Box 248 - Columbus, NJ 08022

Sal Quartuccio & Bob Keenan - Publishers

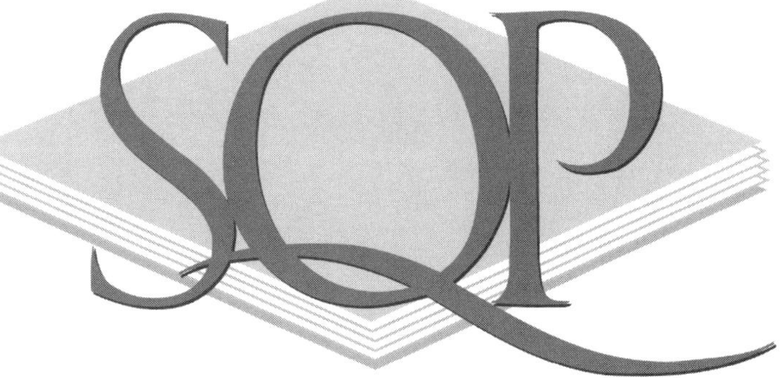

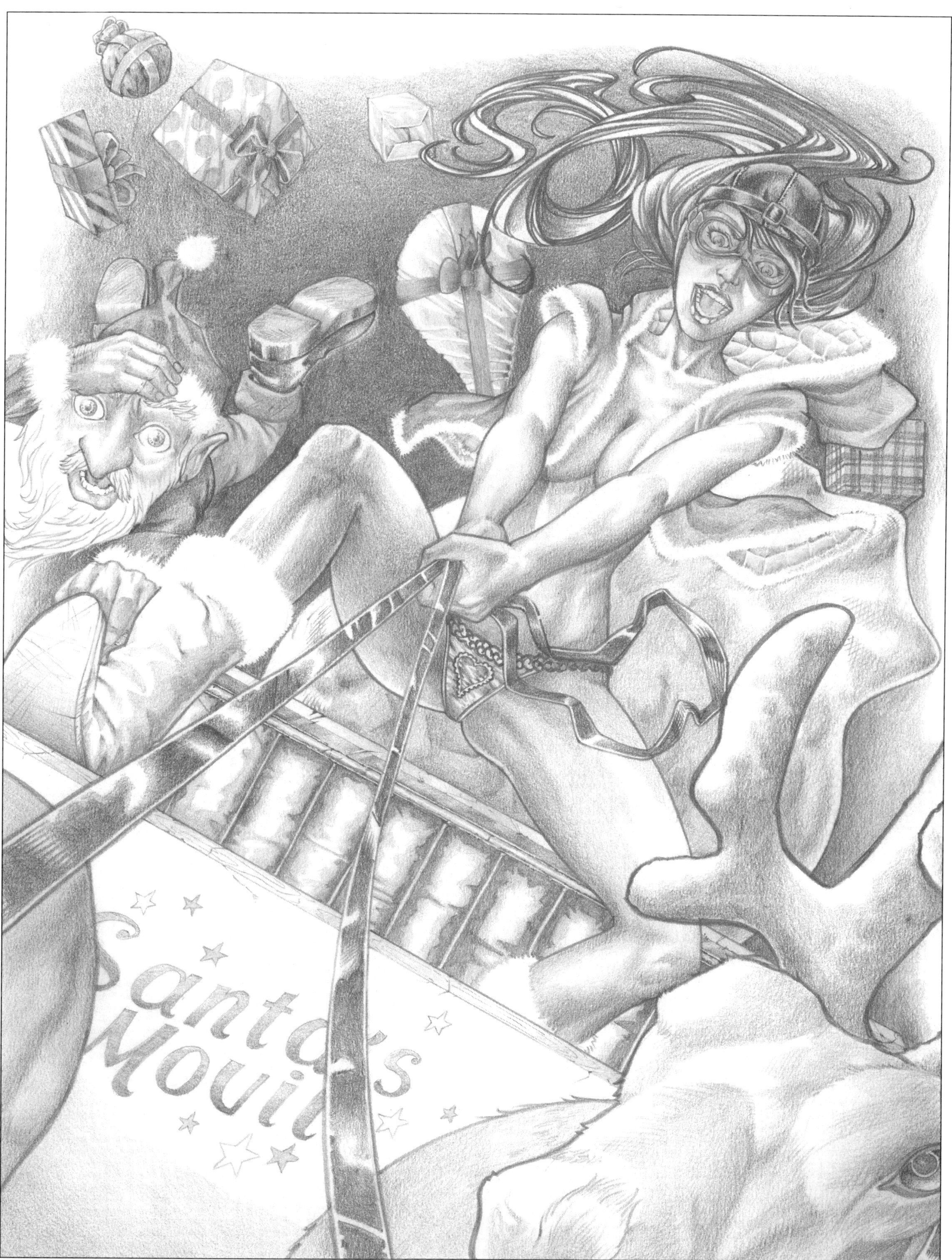

Emiliano Urdinola

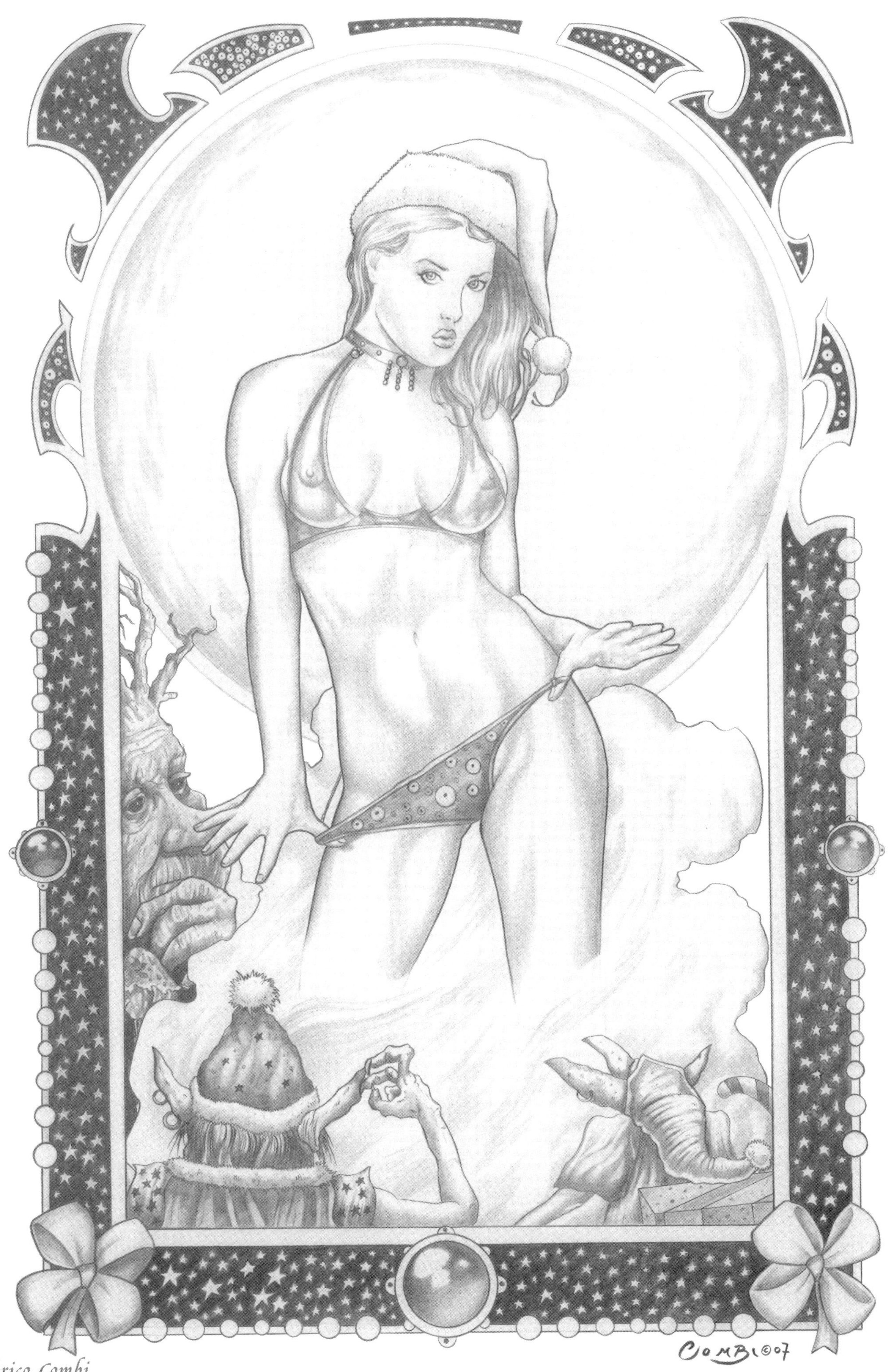

Federico Combi

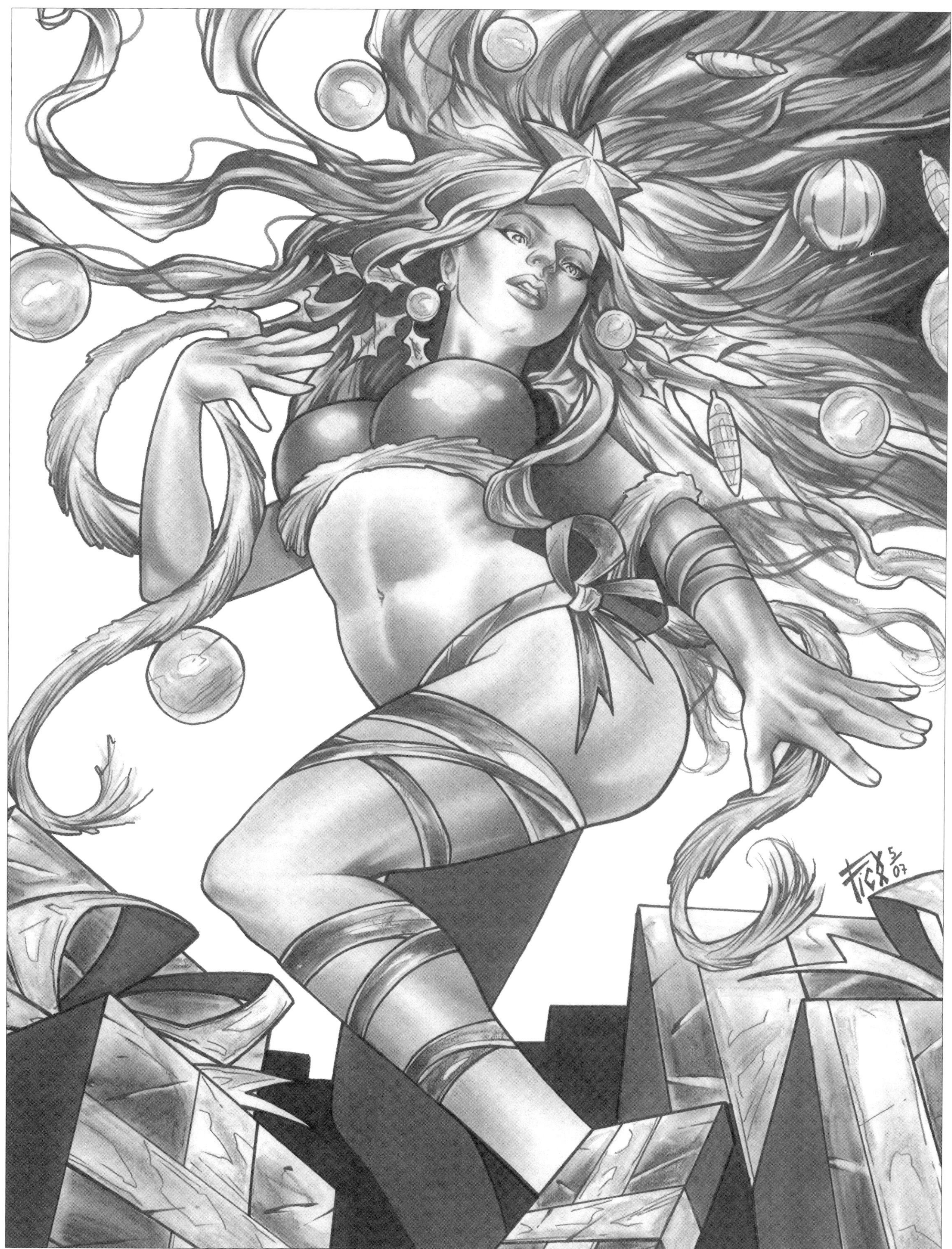

Federico Ossio

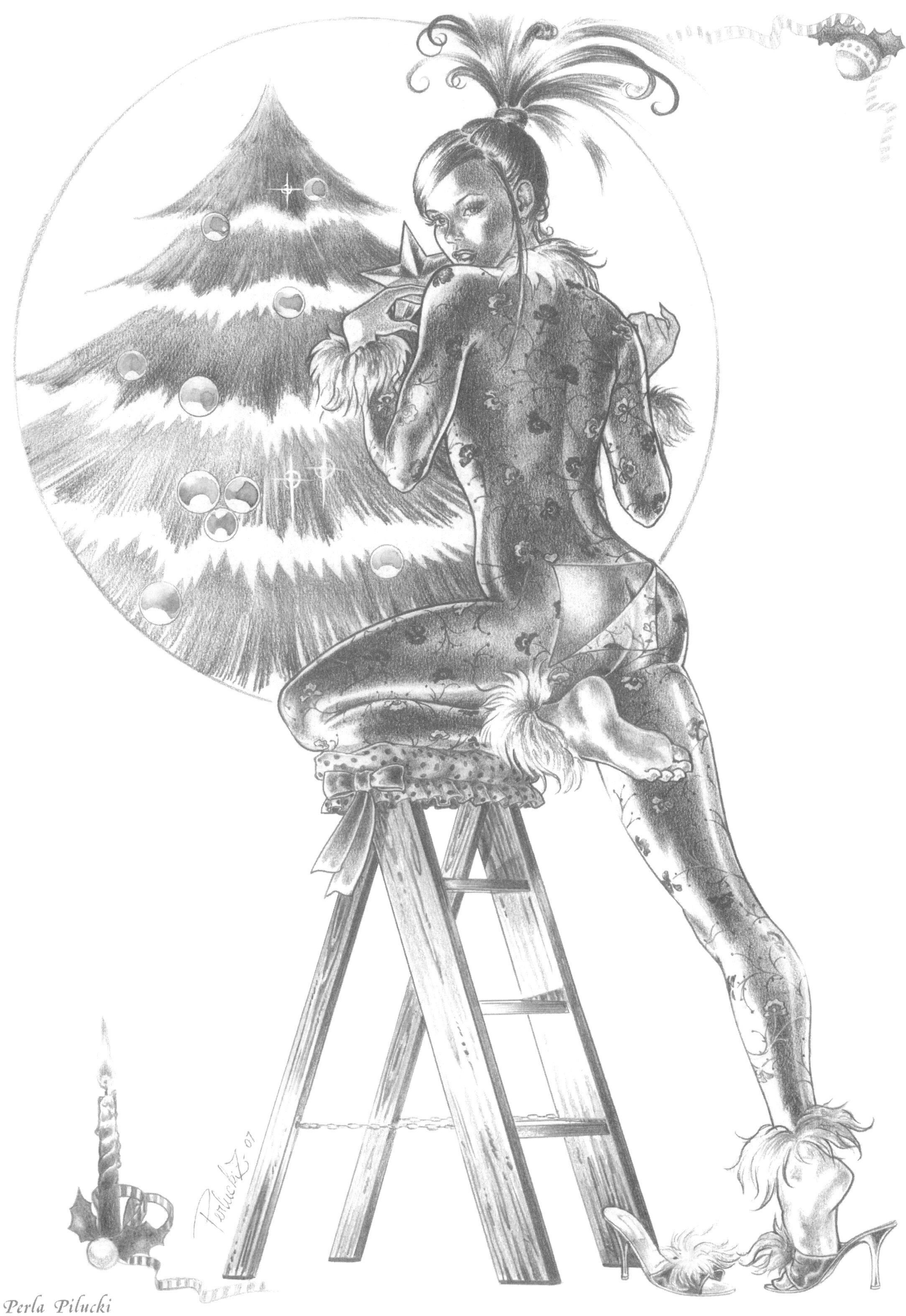

Perla Pilucki

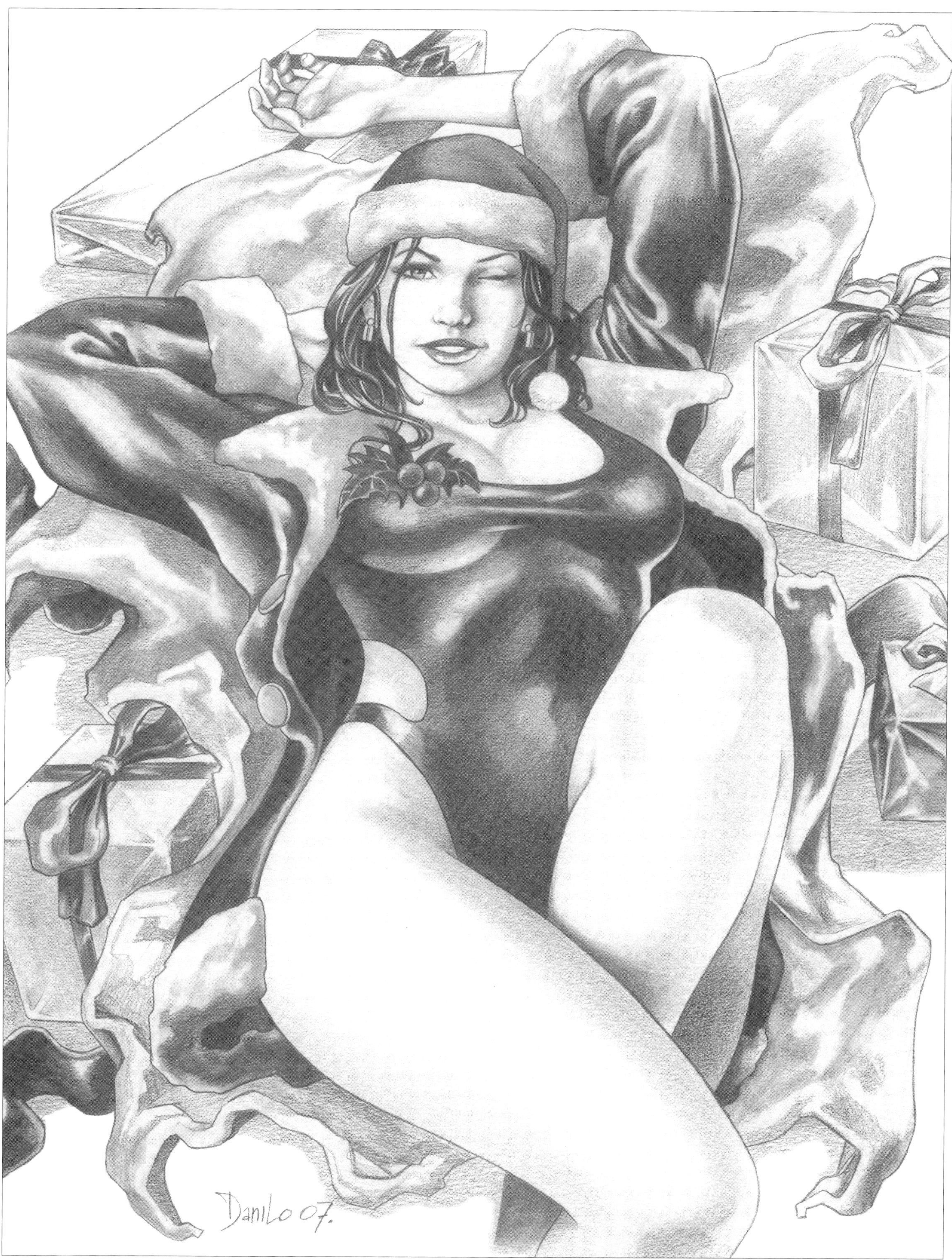

Danilo Guida

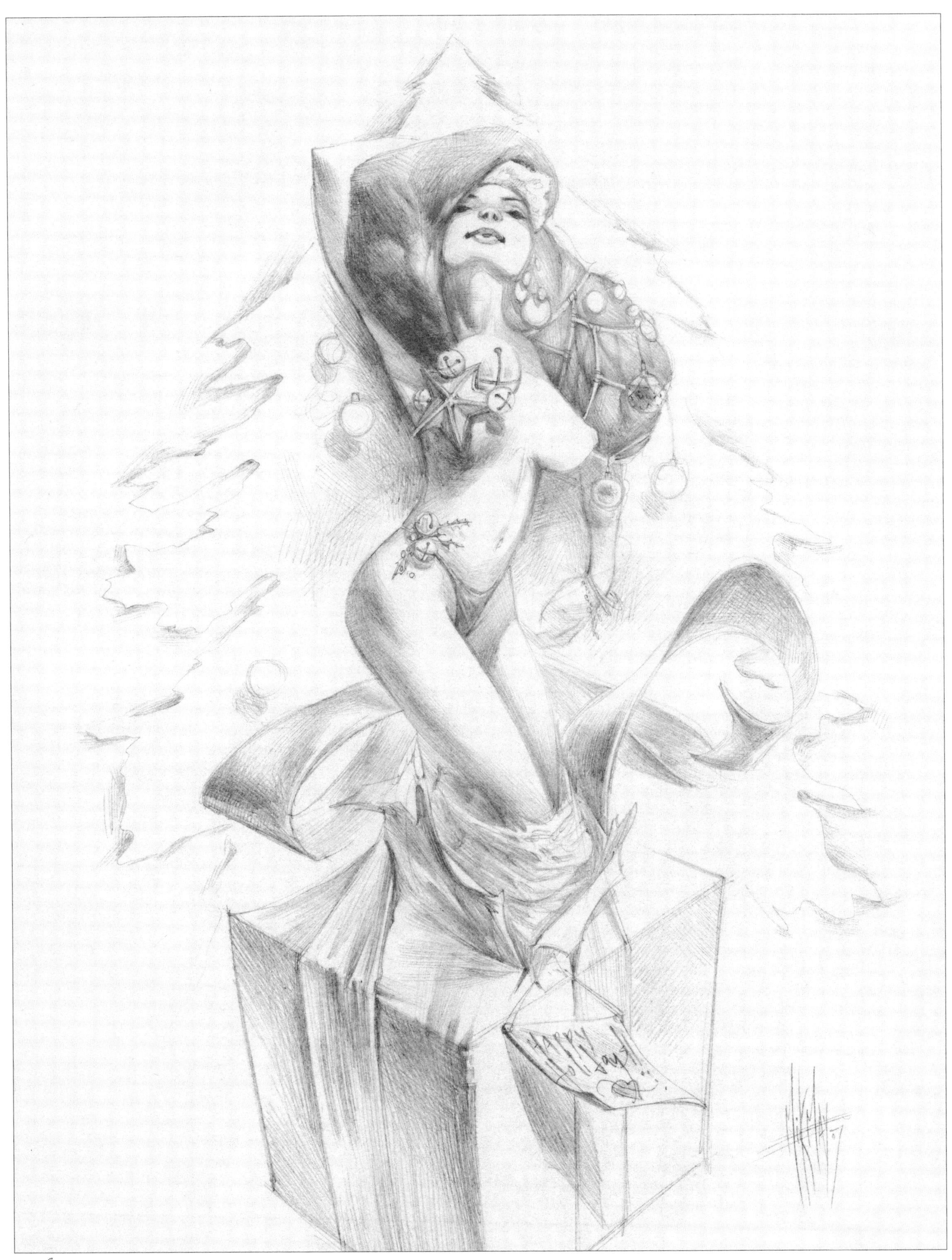

Mike May

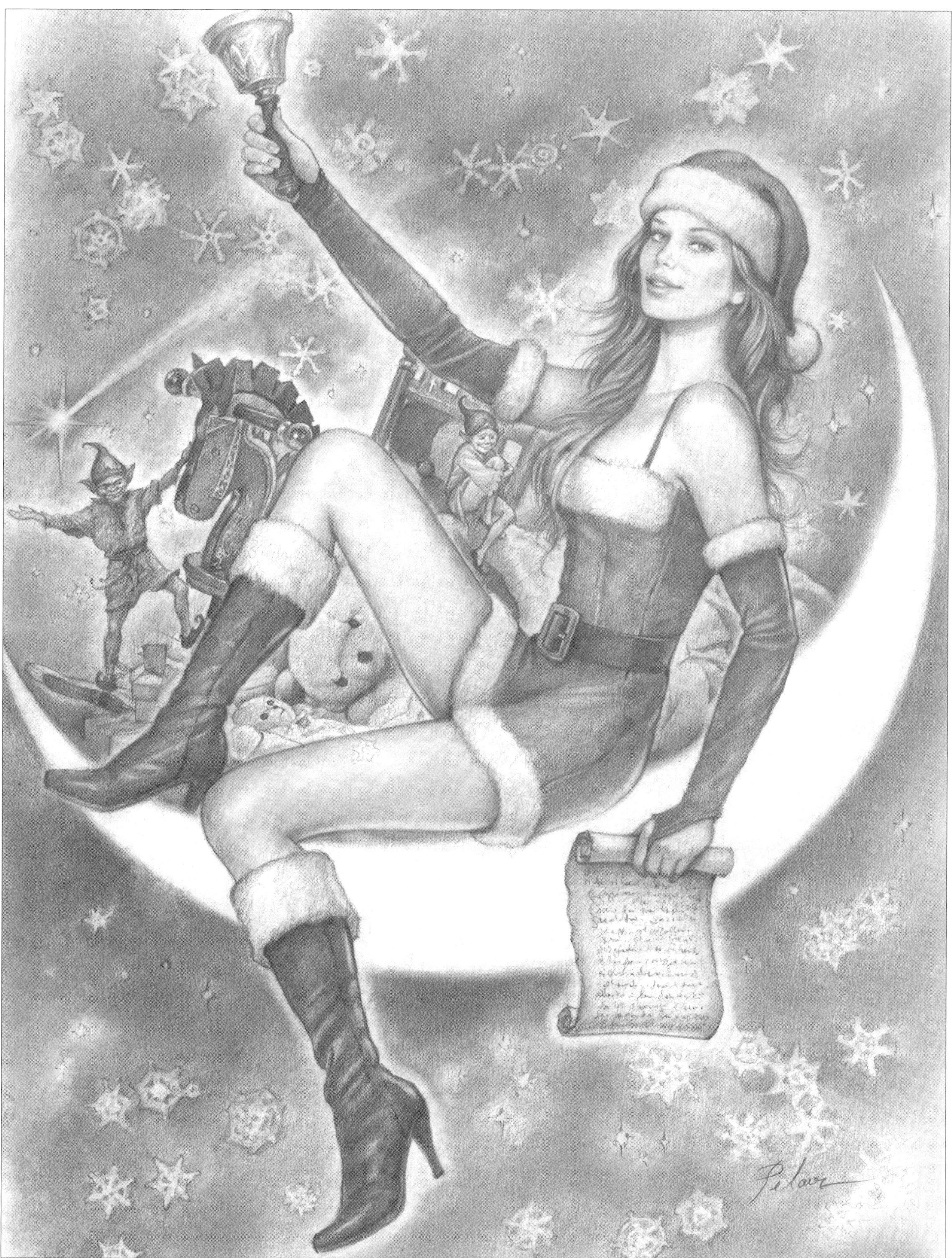

Pelaez

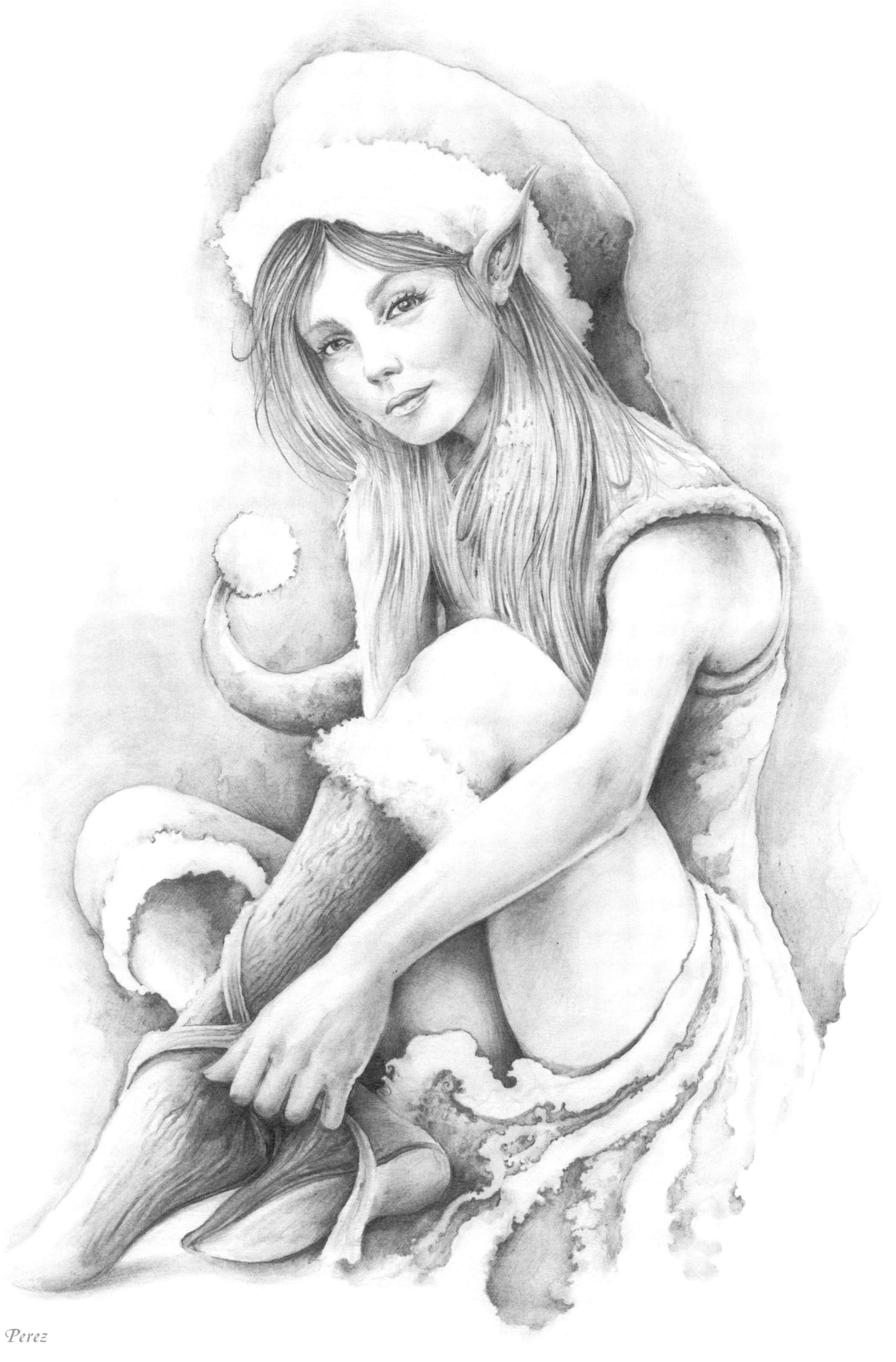

Aldo Perez

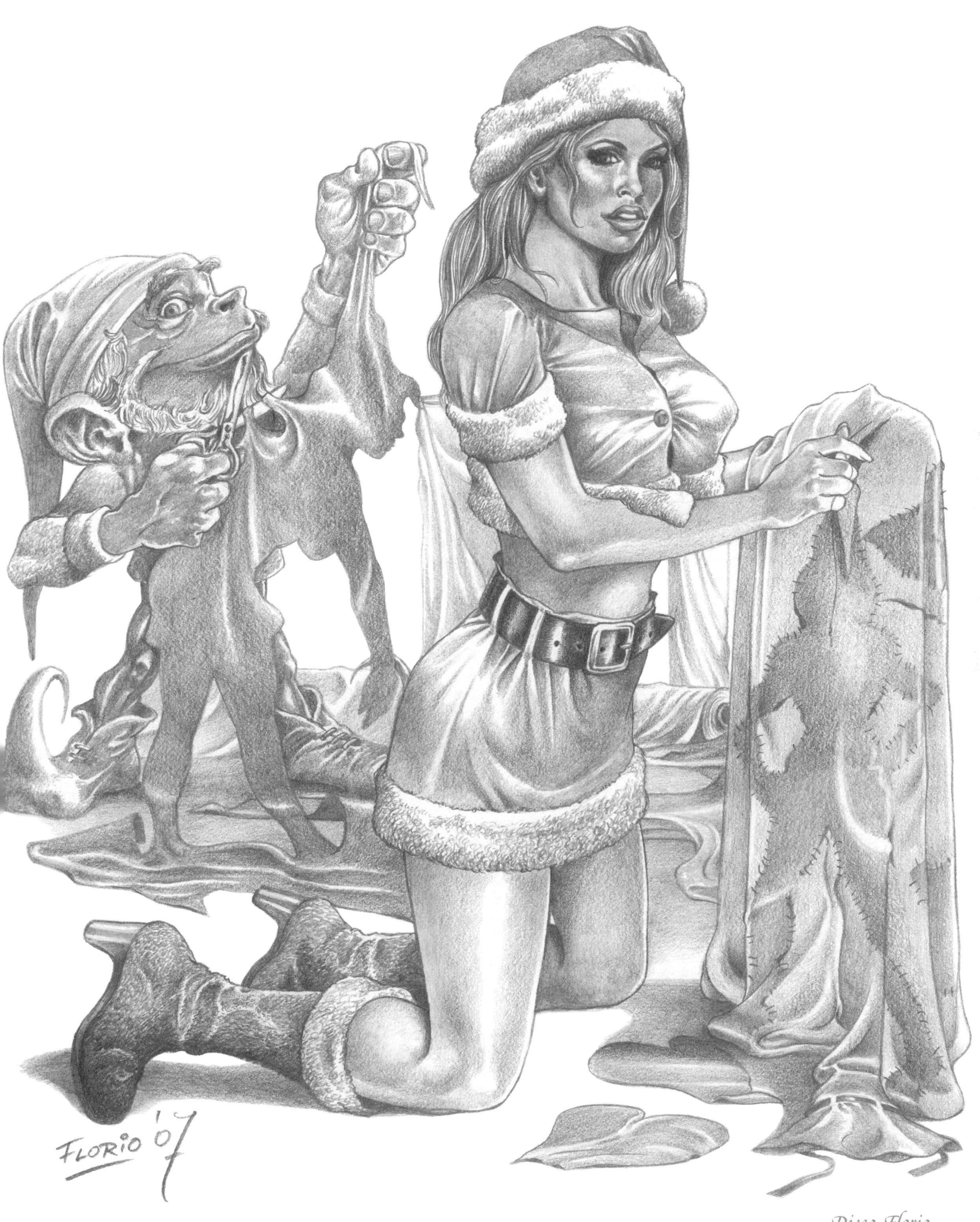

Diego Florio

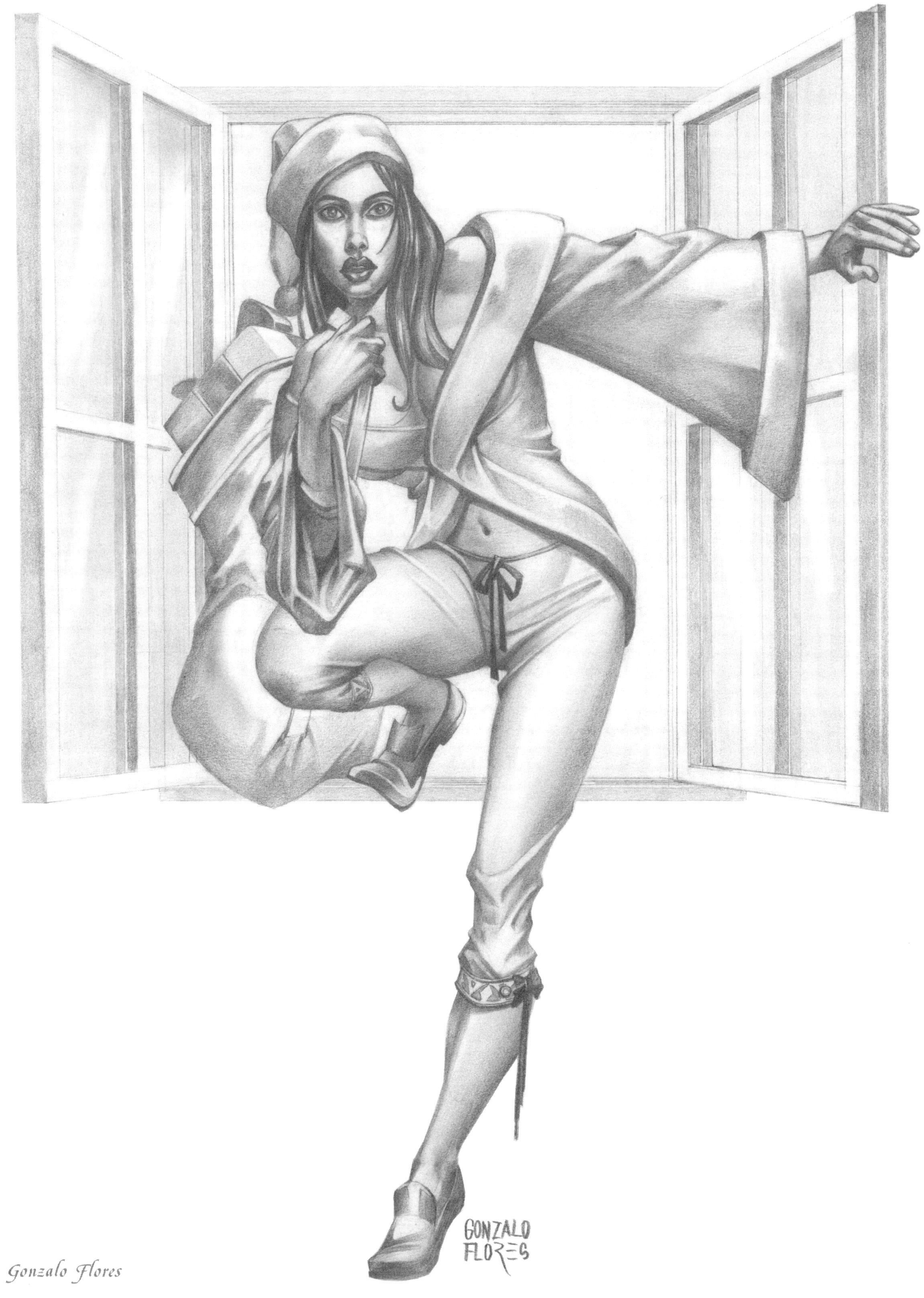

Gonzalo Flores

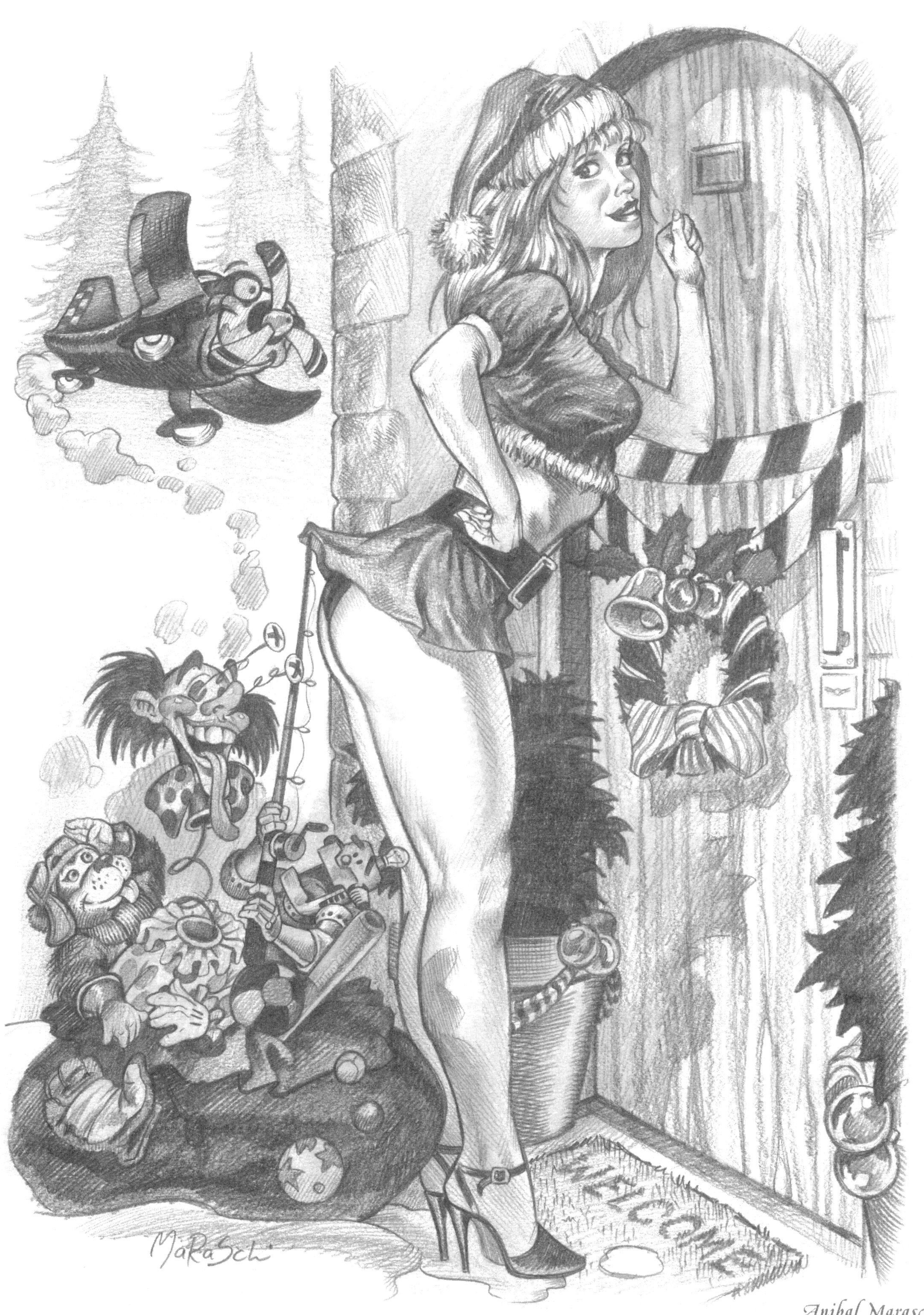

Anibal Maraschi

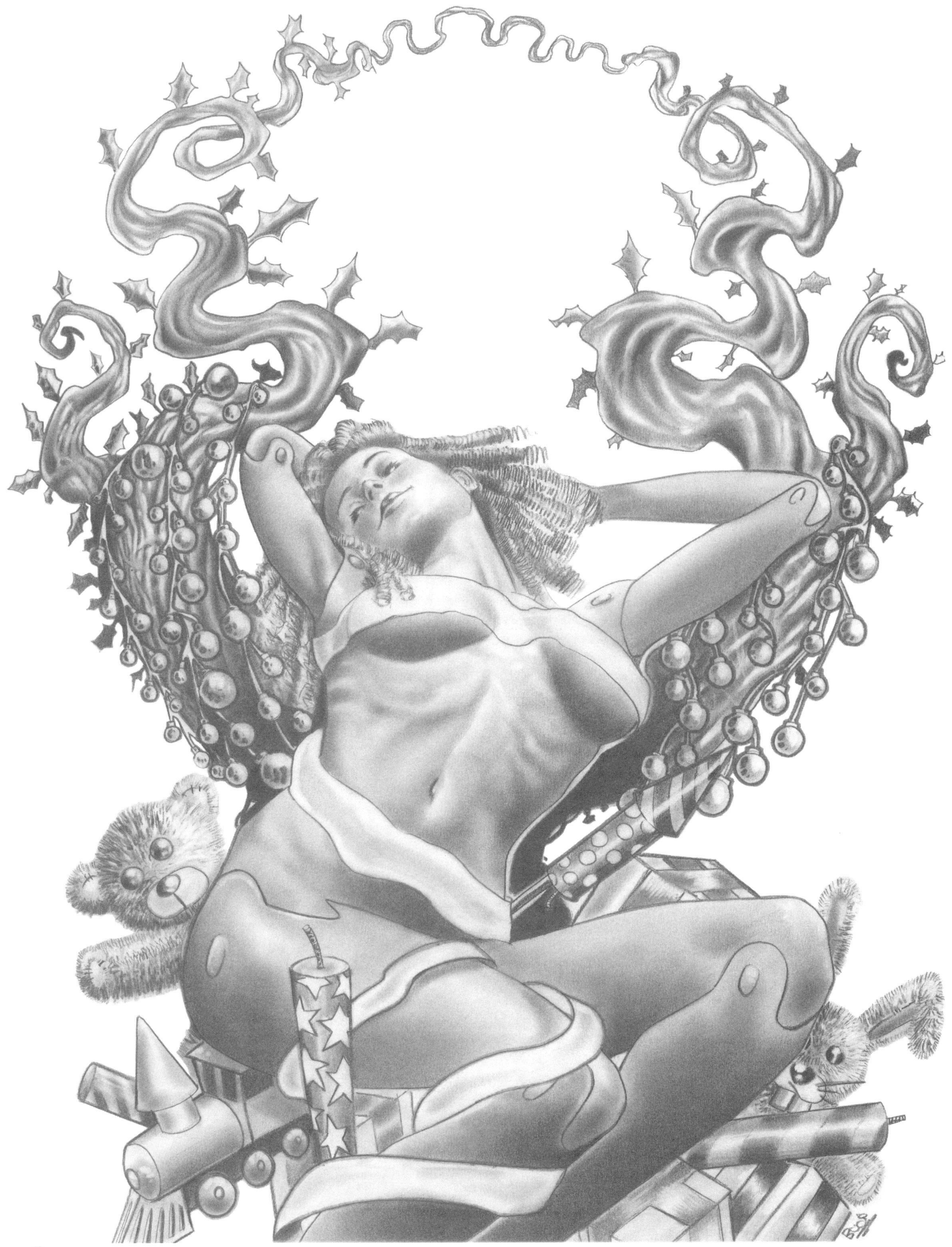

Luis Buci

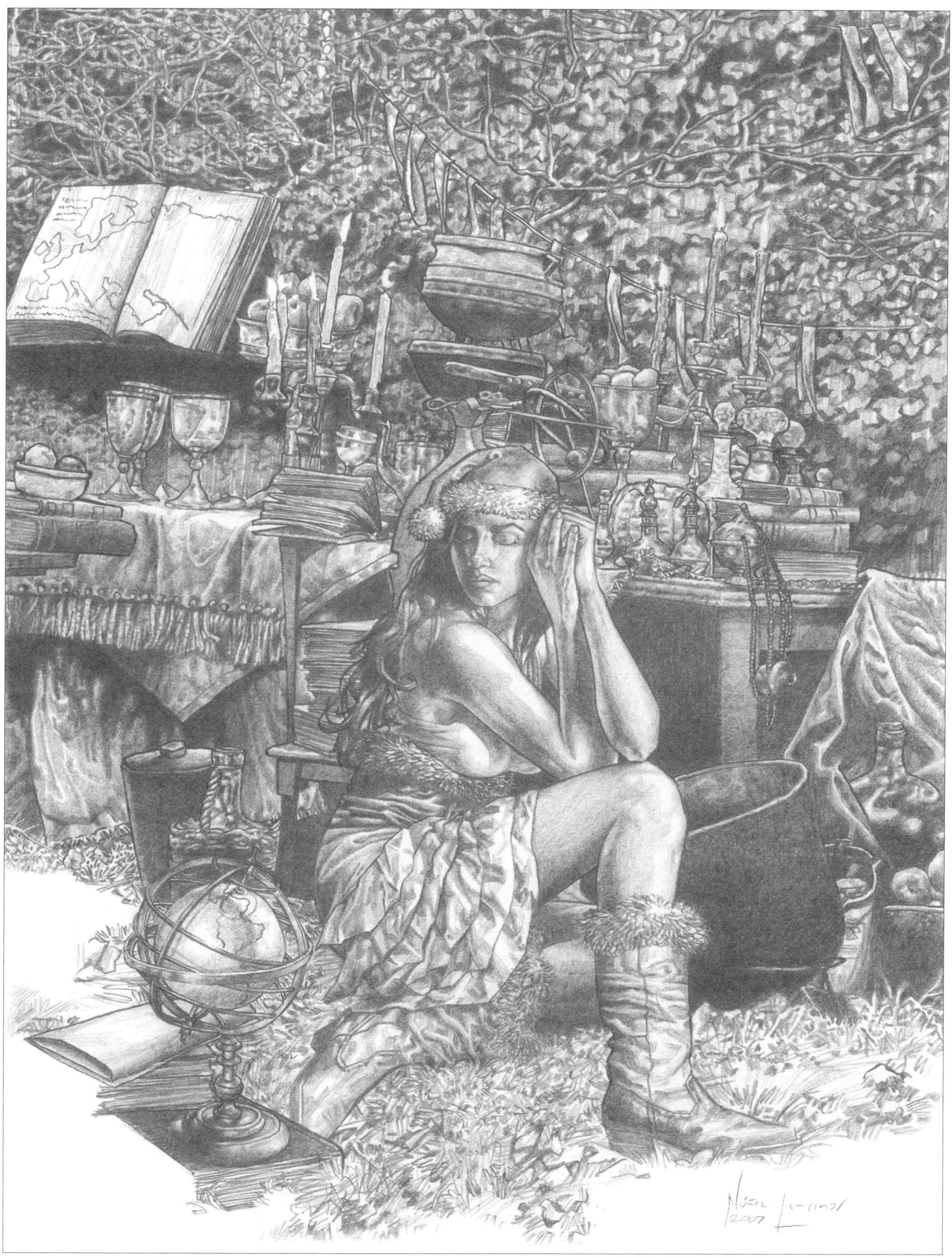

Juan Lencina

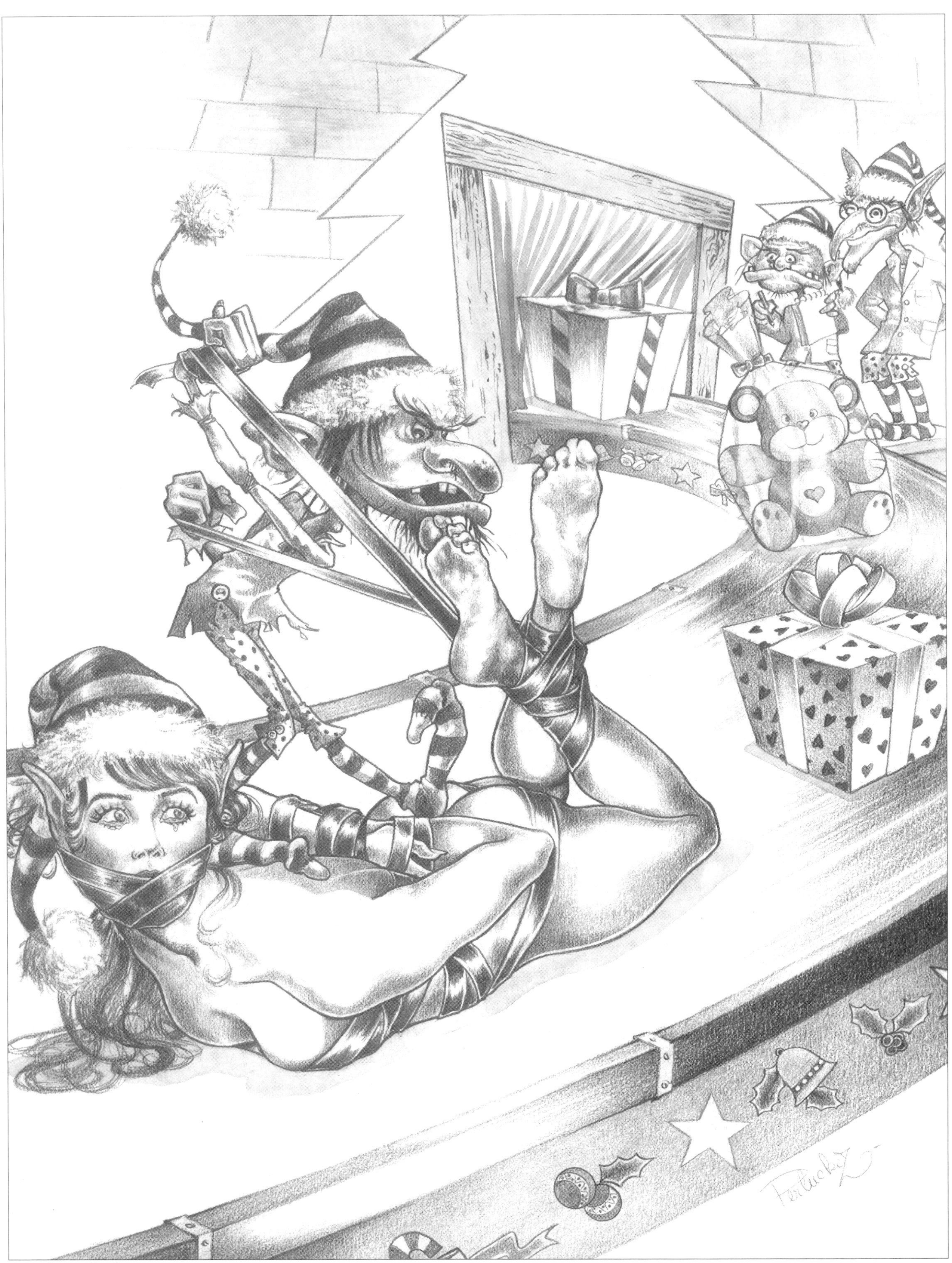

Perla Pilucki

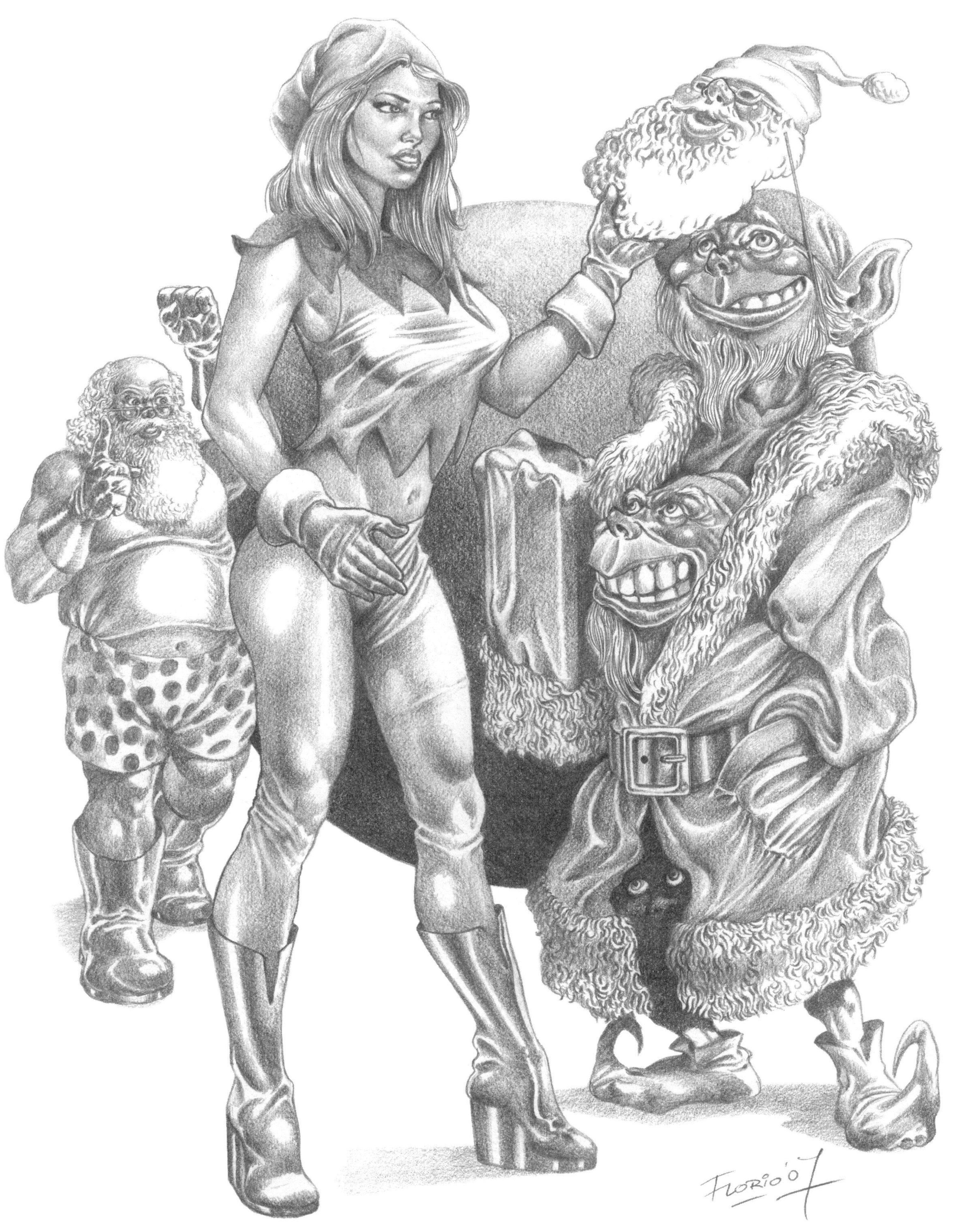

Diego Florio

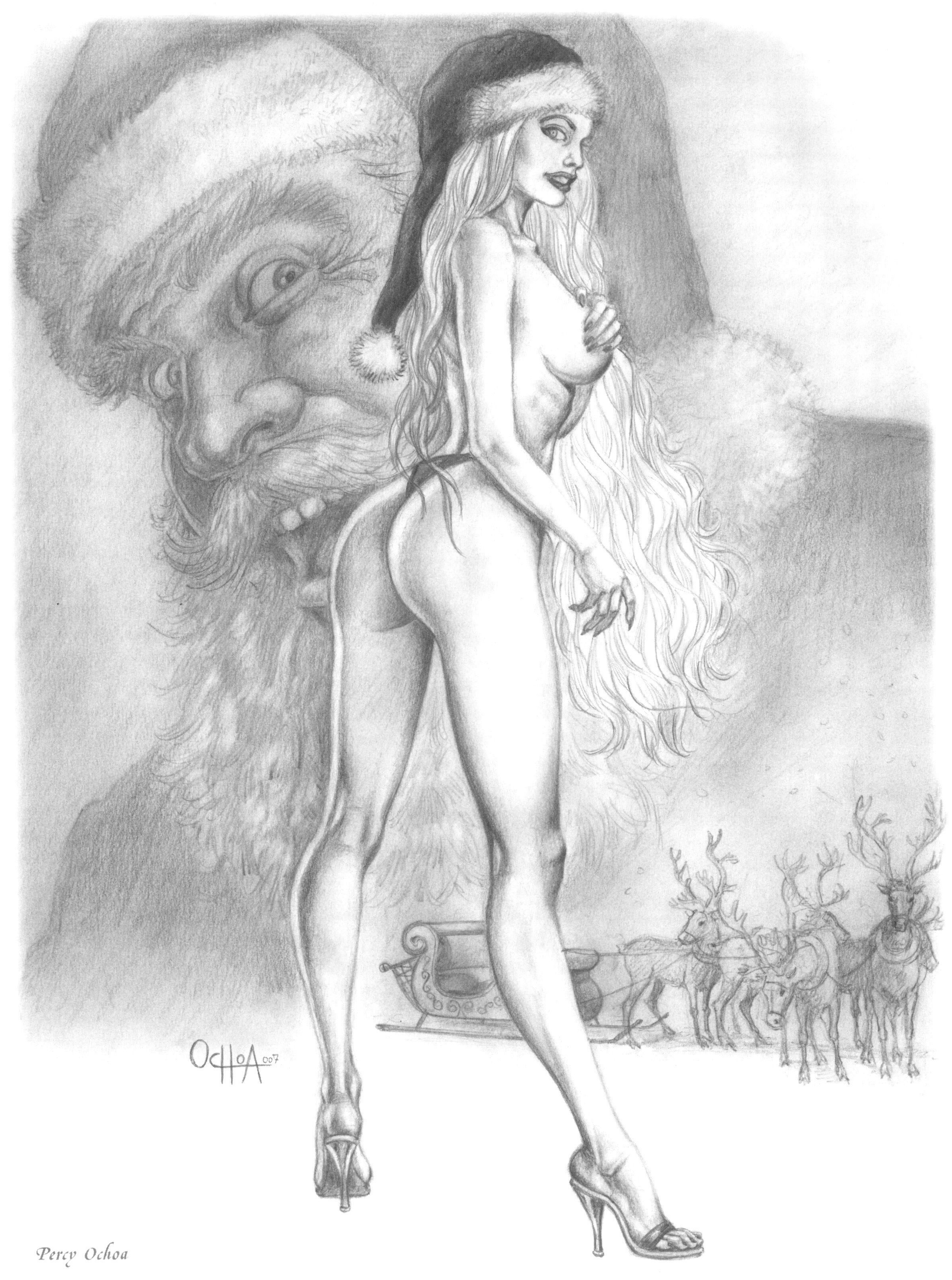

Percy Ochoa

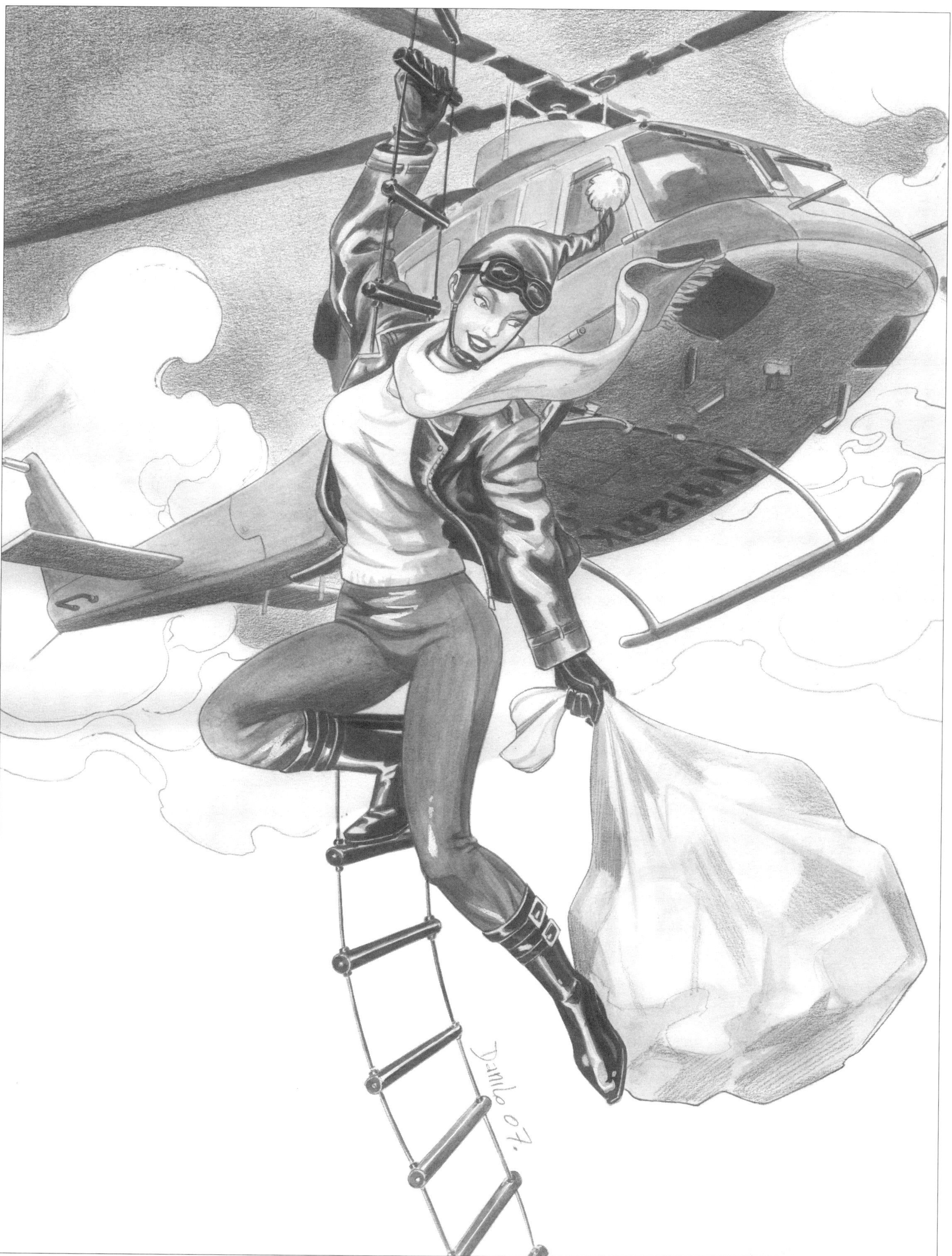

Danilo Guida

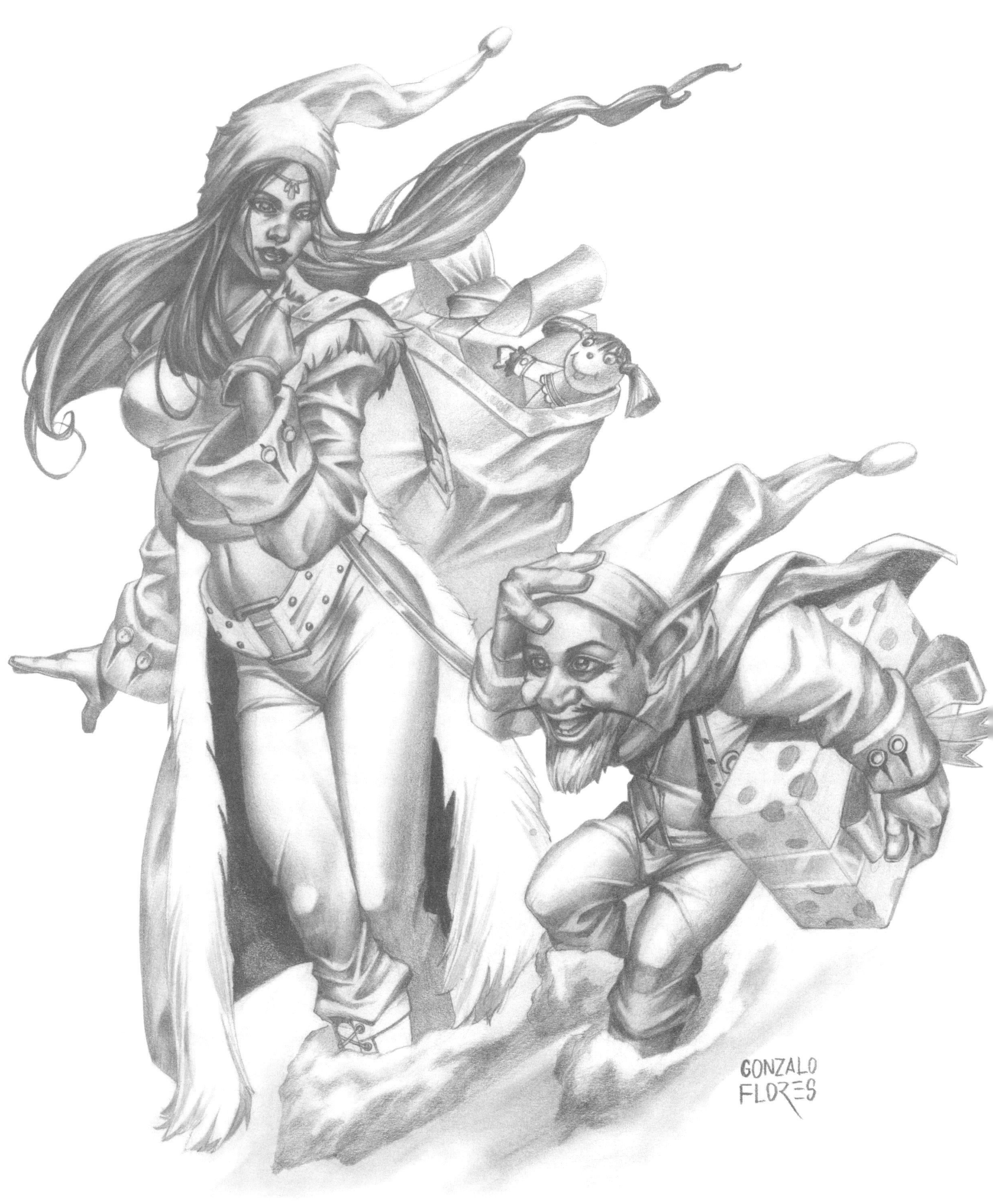

Gonzalo Flores

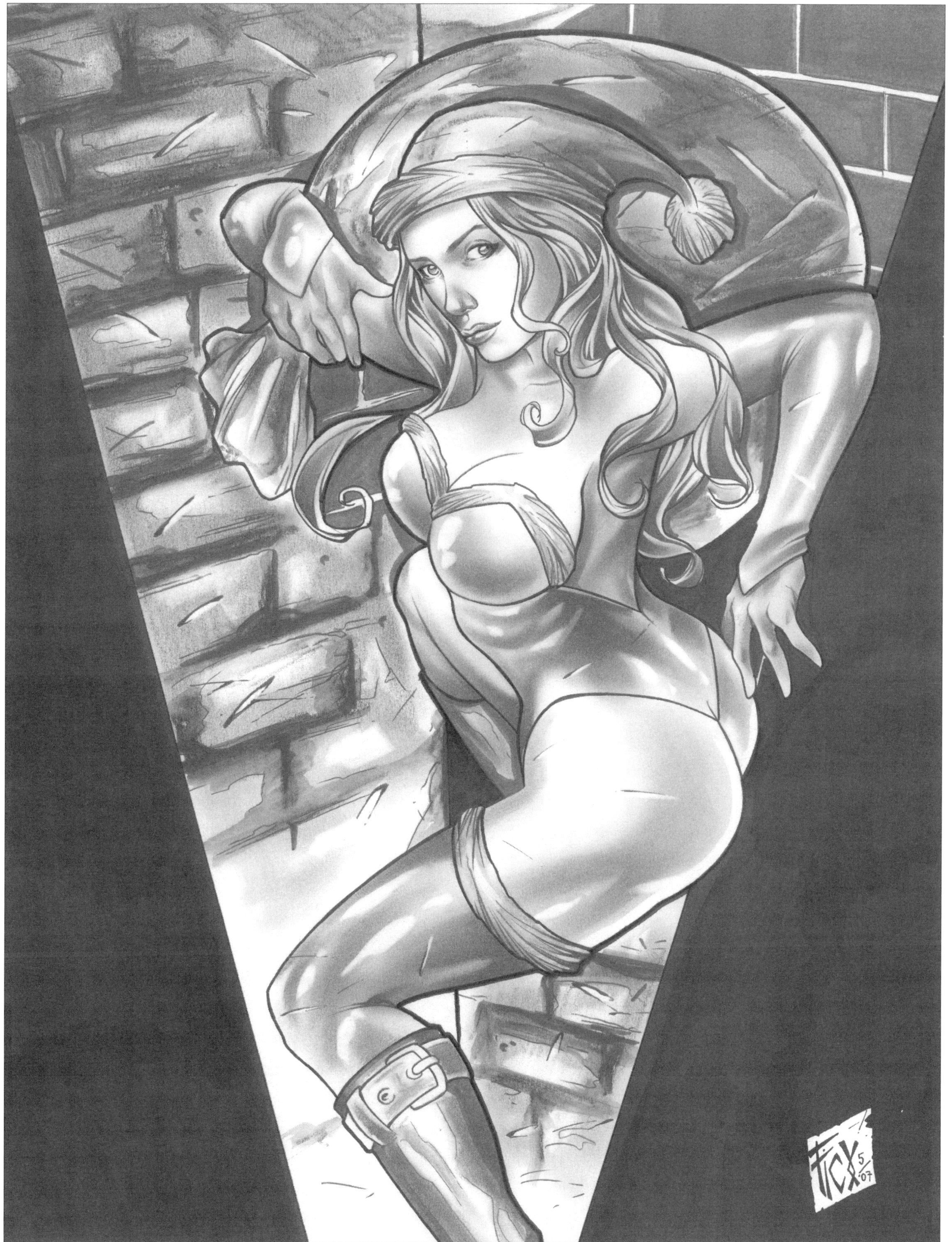

Federico Ossio

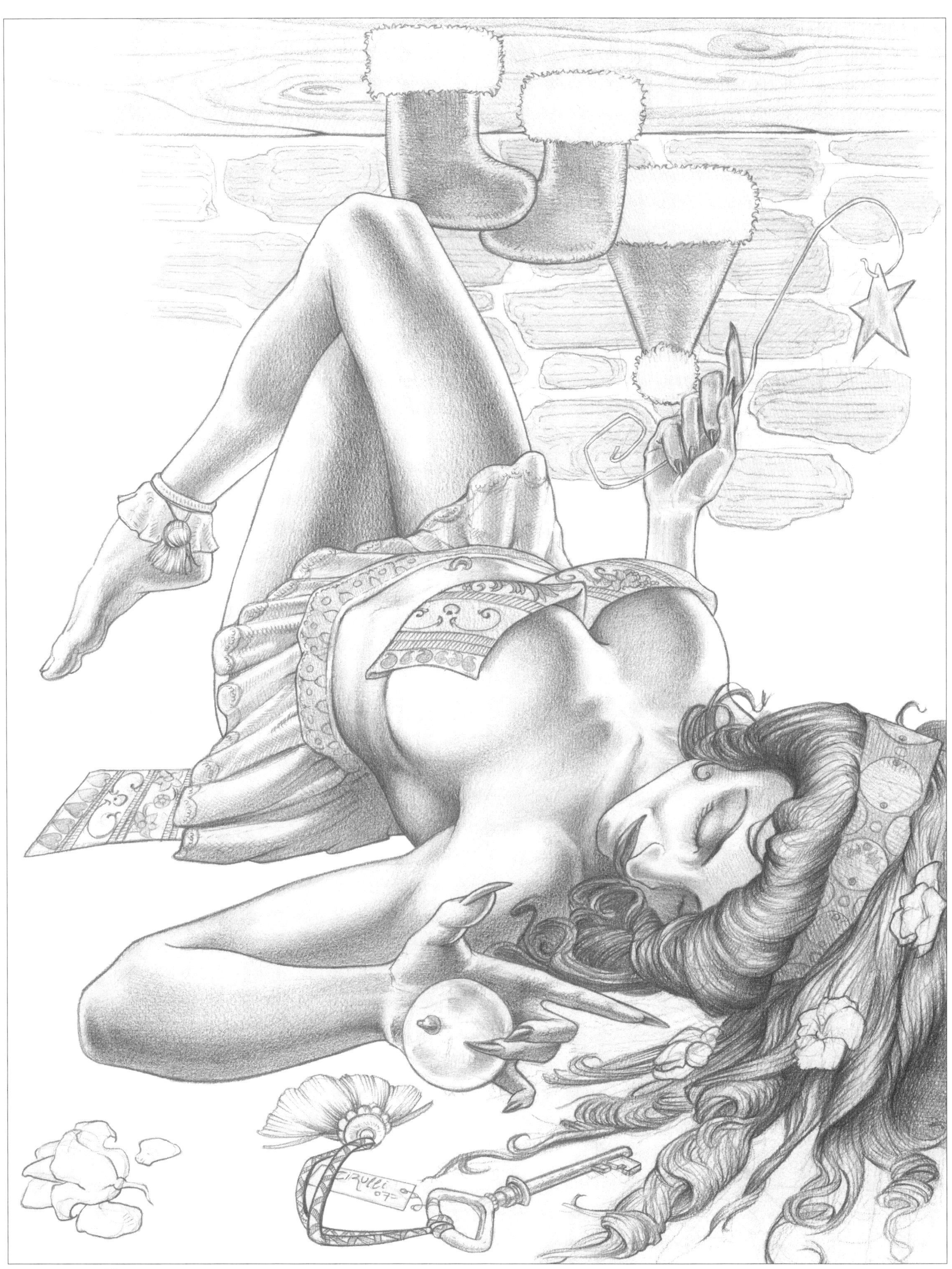

Diego Cirulli

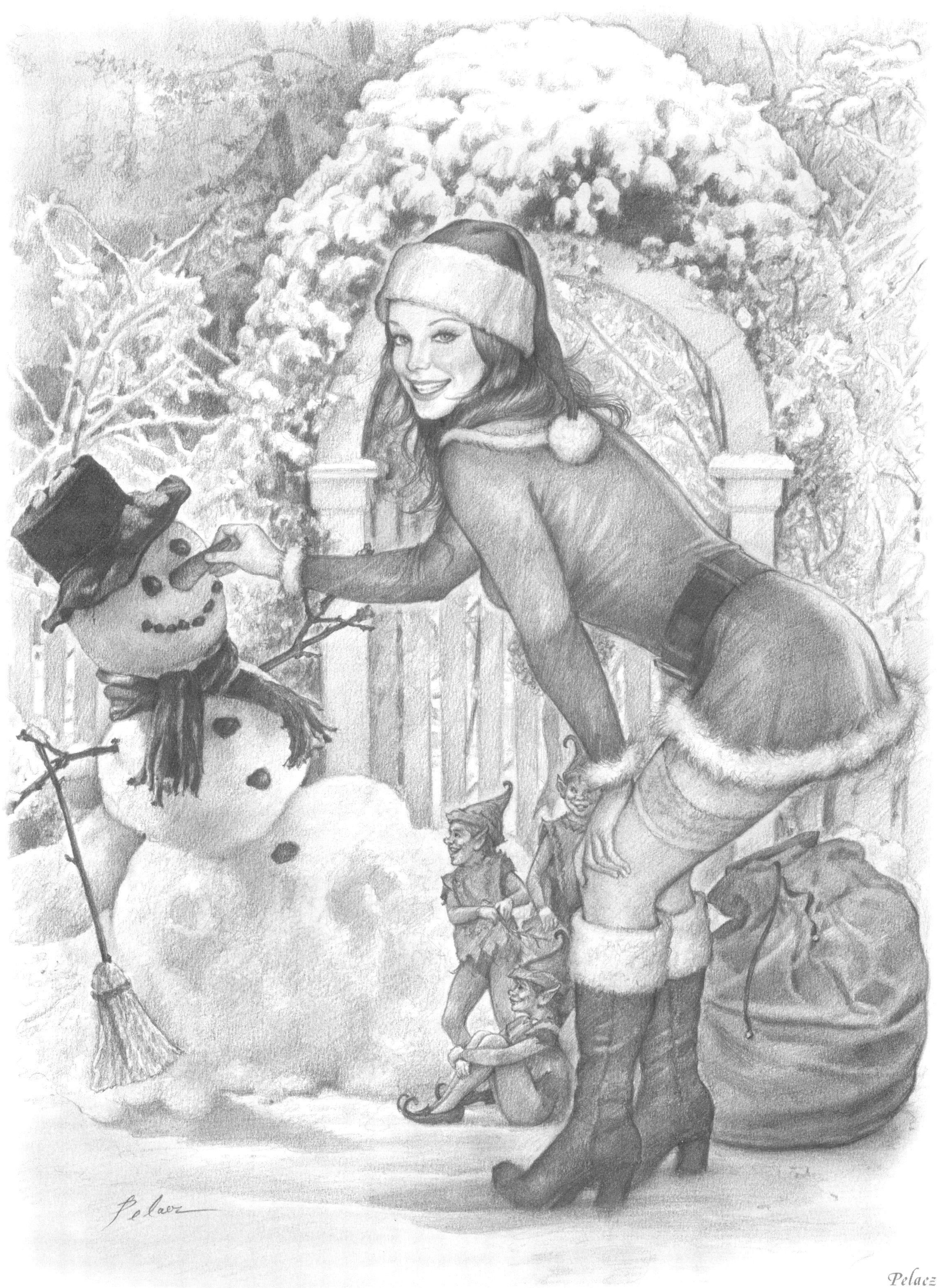

Pelaez

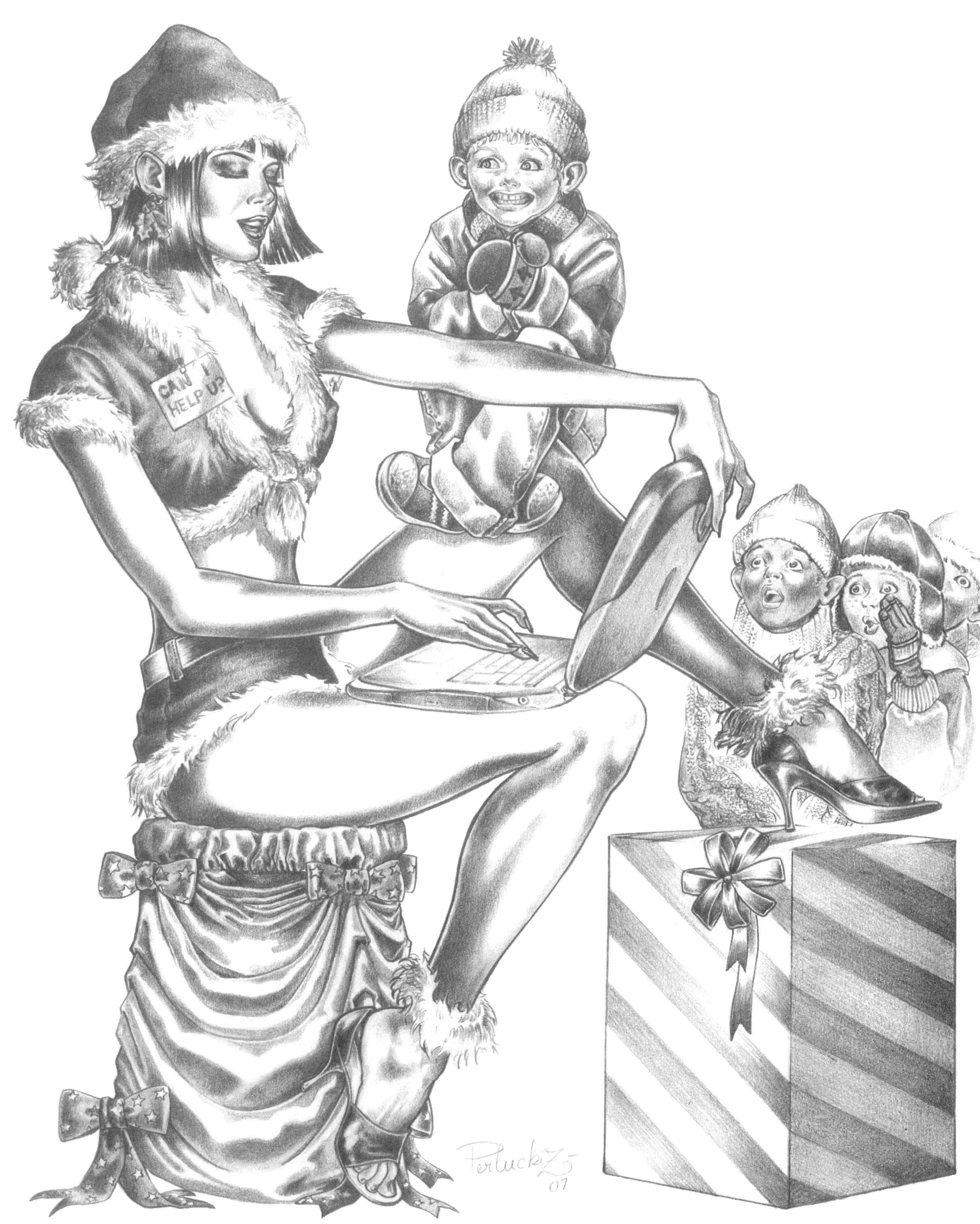

Perla Pilucki

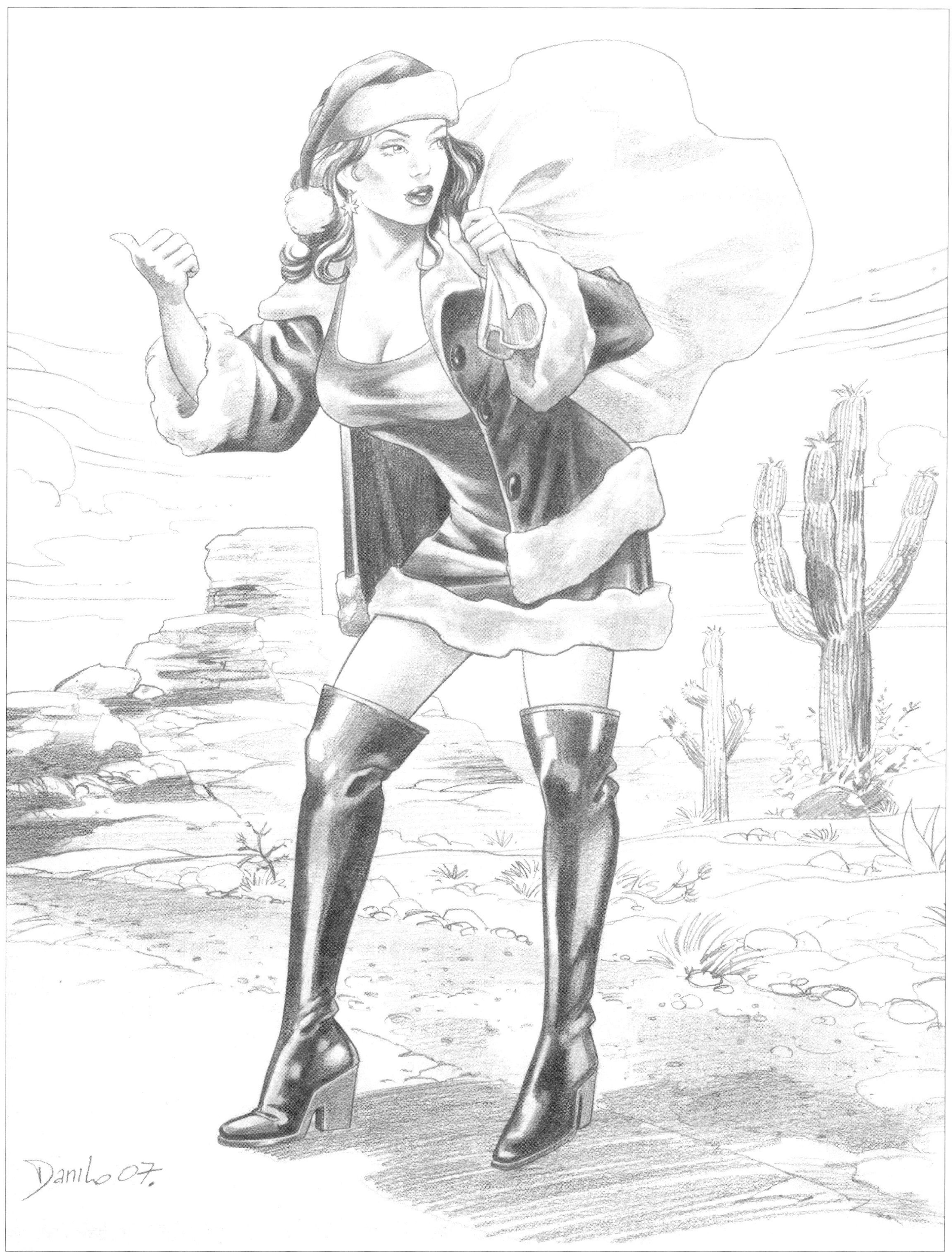

Danilo Guida

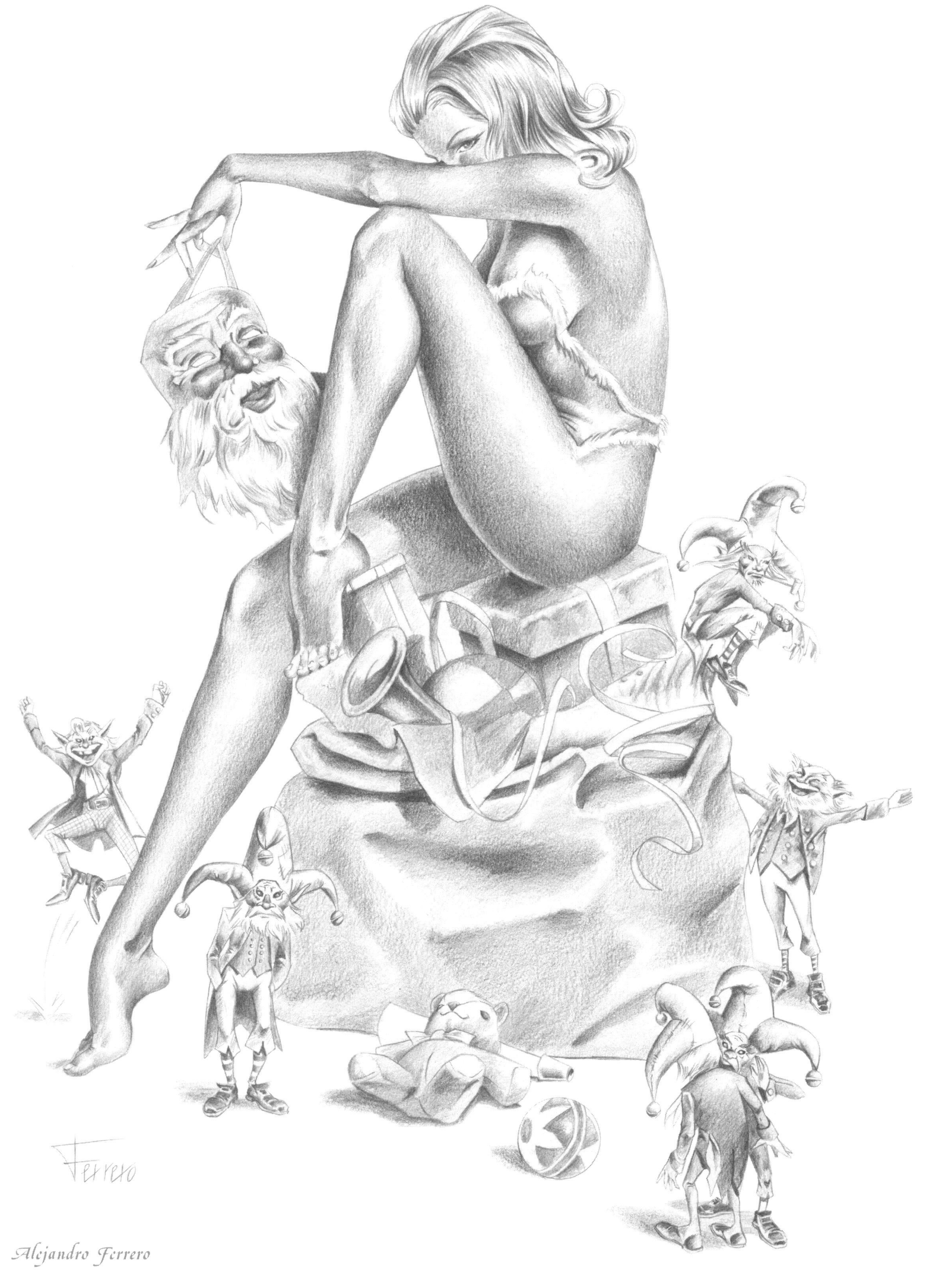

Alejandro Ferrero

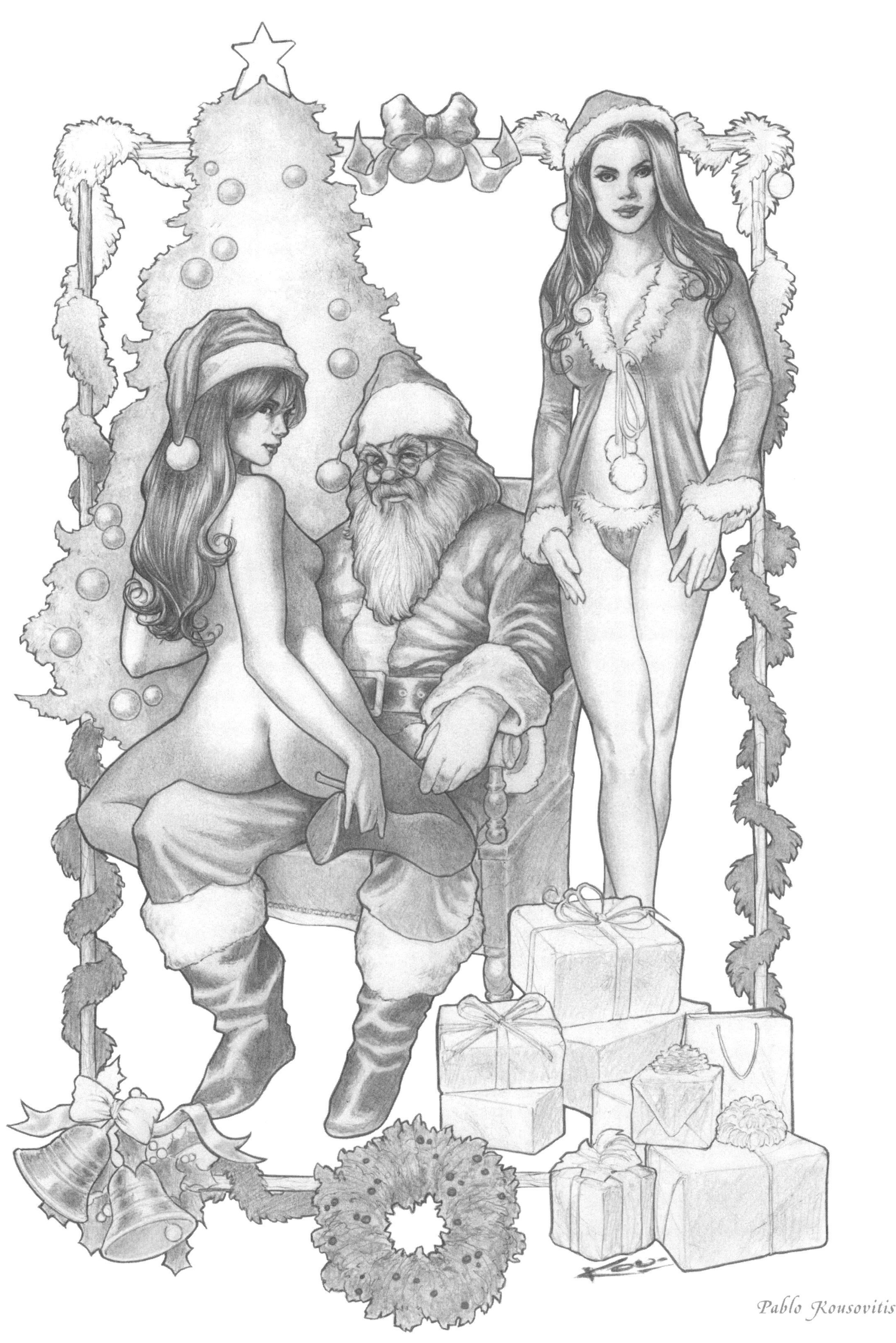

Pablo Kousovitis

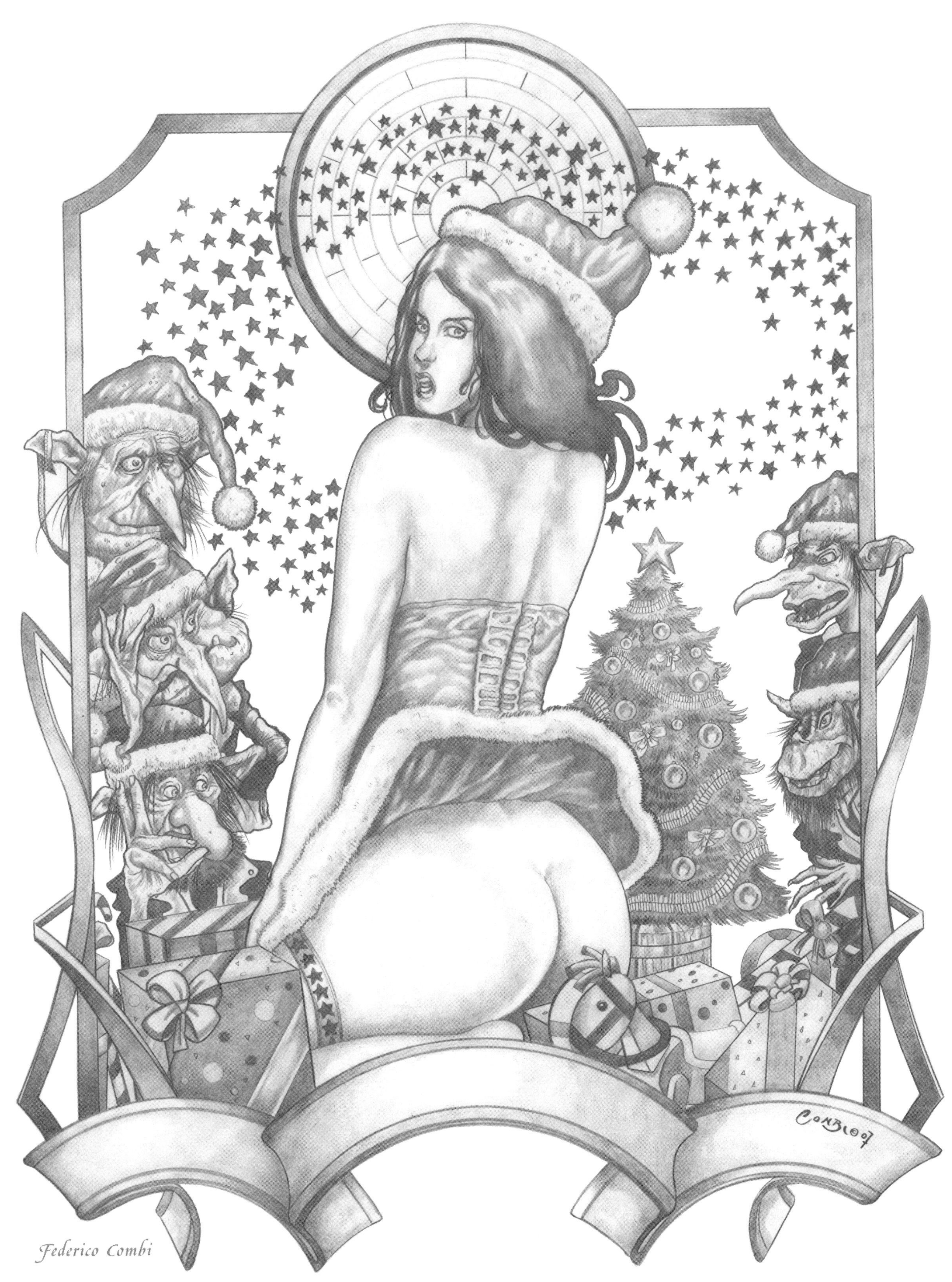

Federico Combi

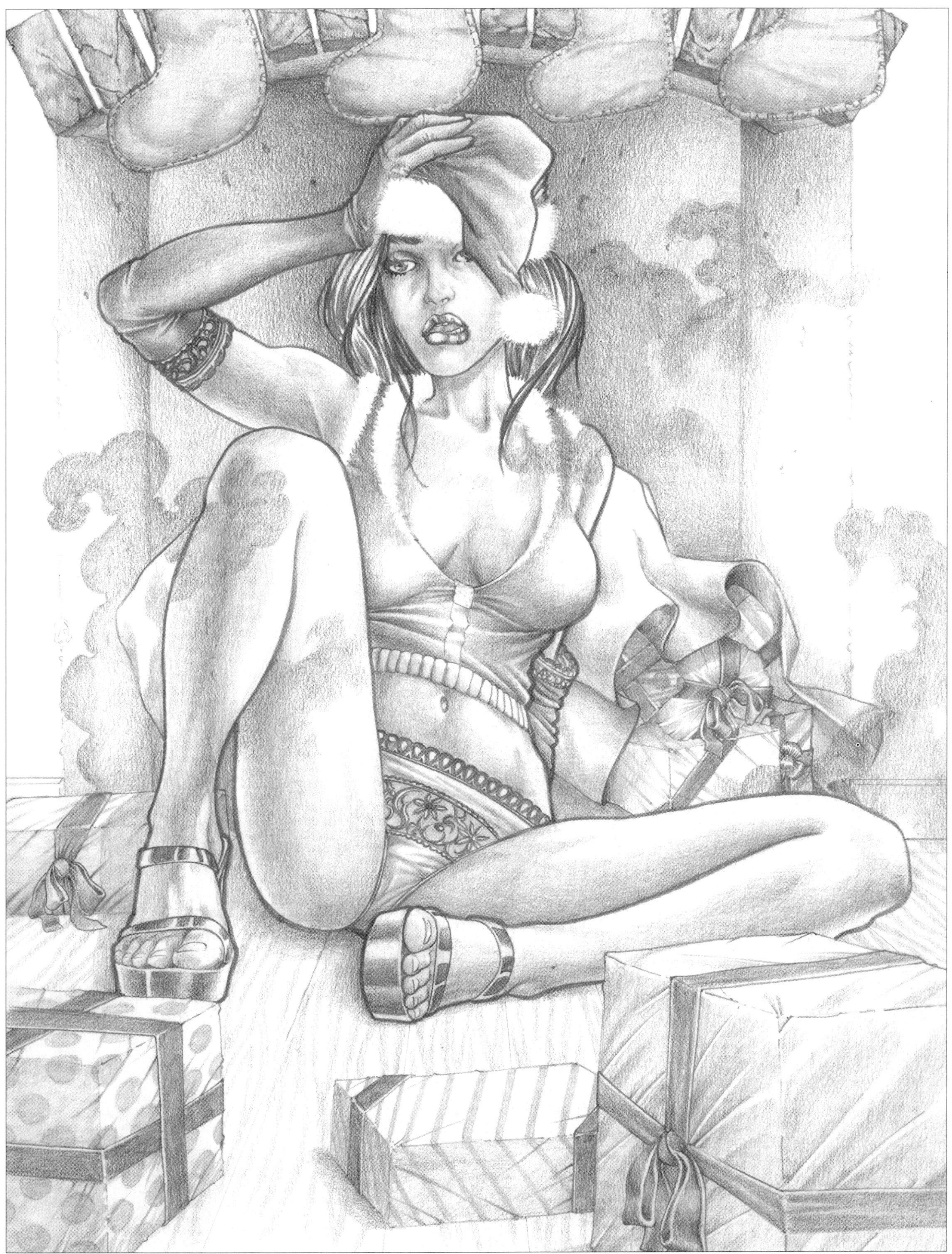

Emiliano Urdinola

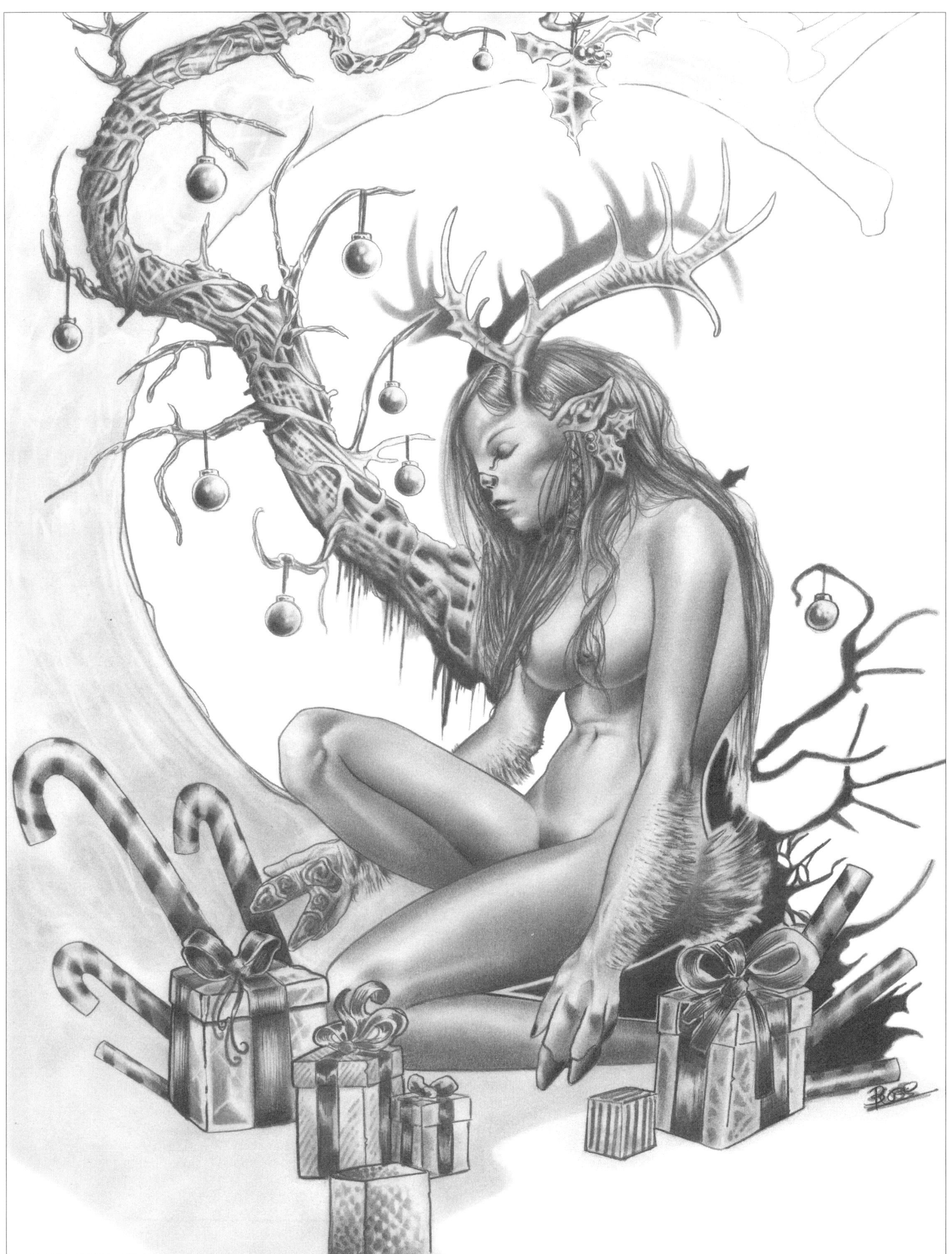

Luis Buci

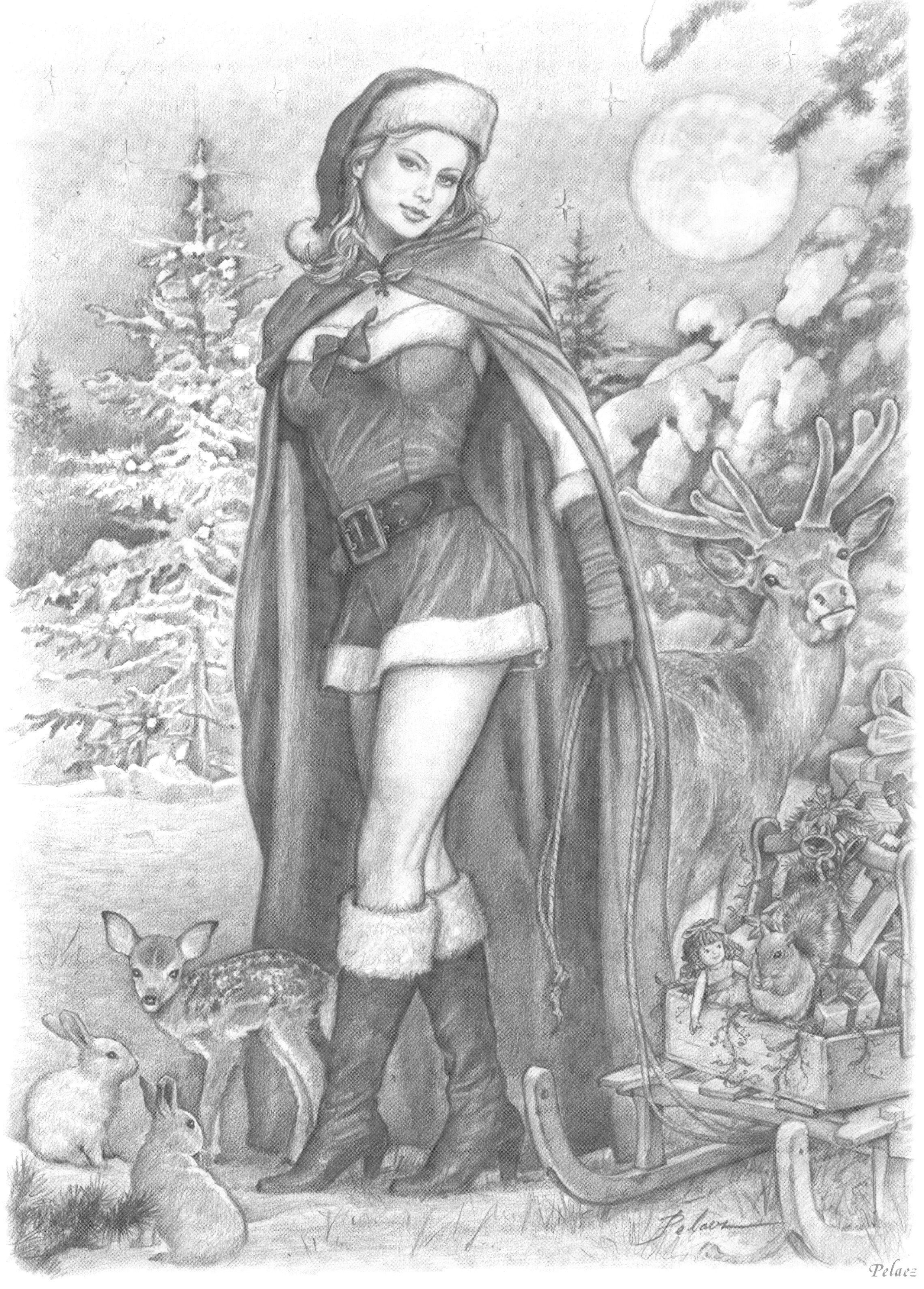

Pelaez

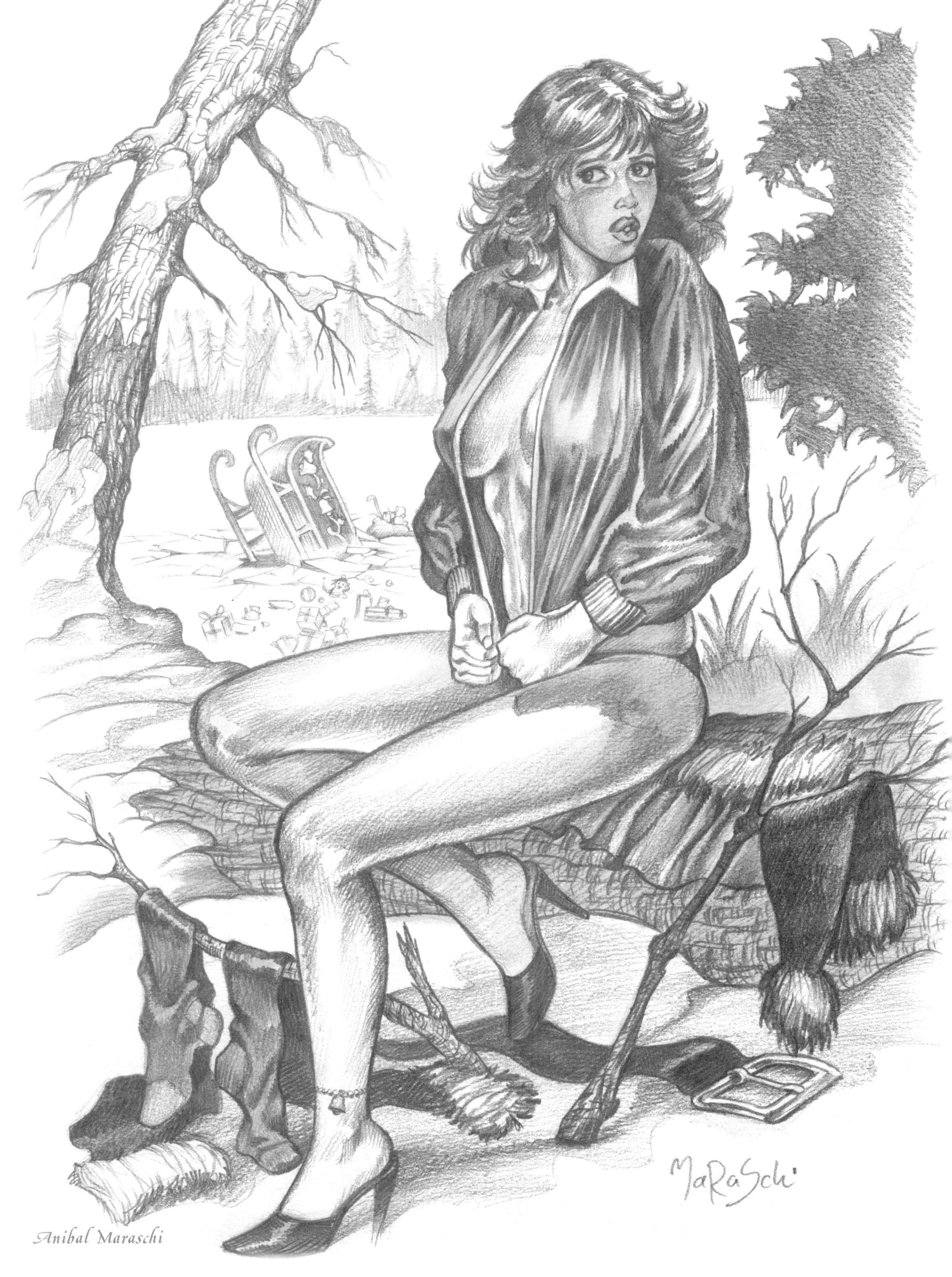

Anibal Maraschi

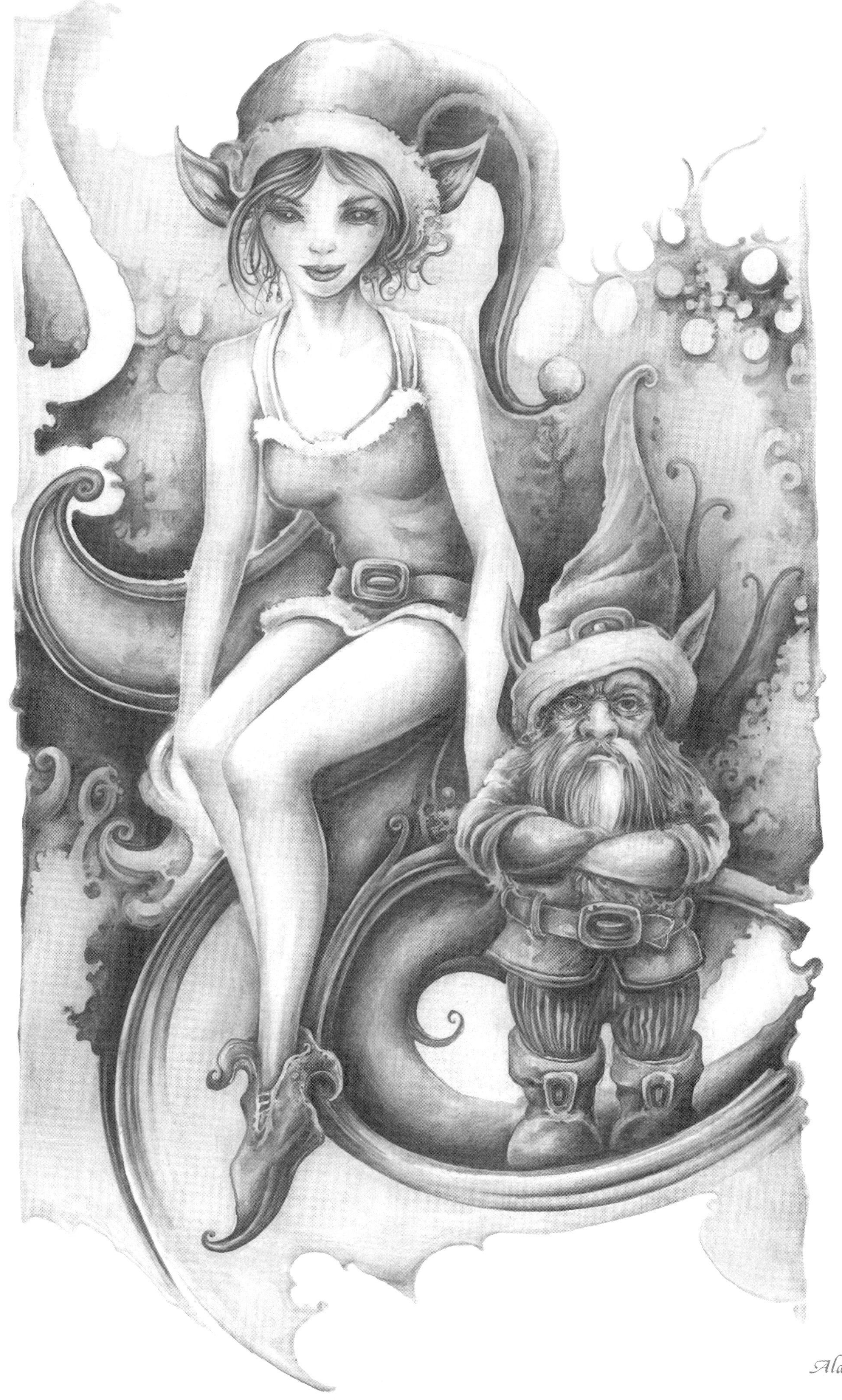

Aldo Perez

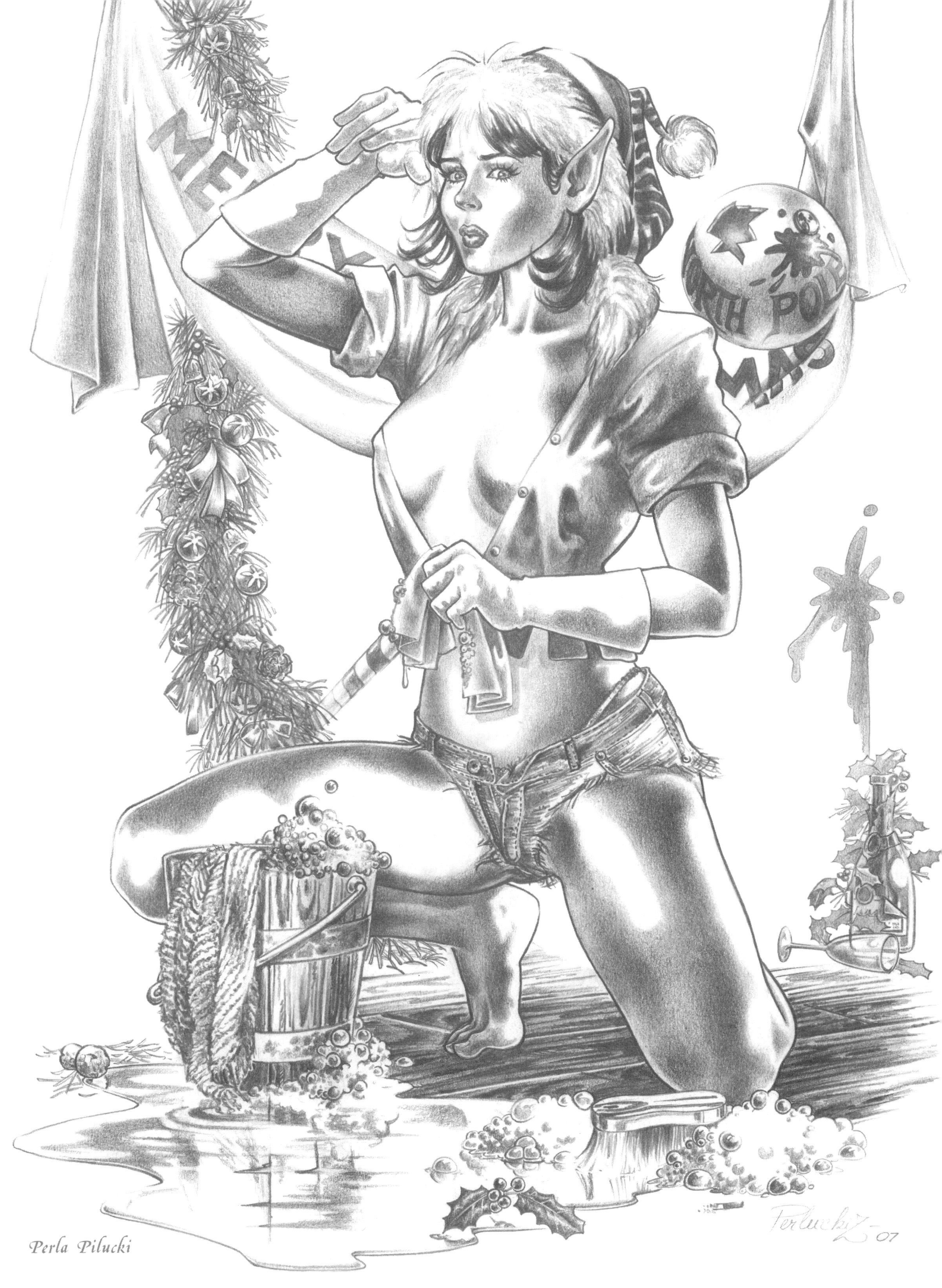

Perla Pilucki

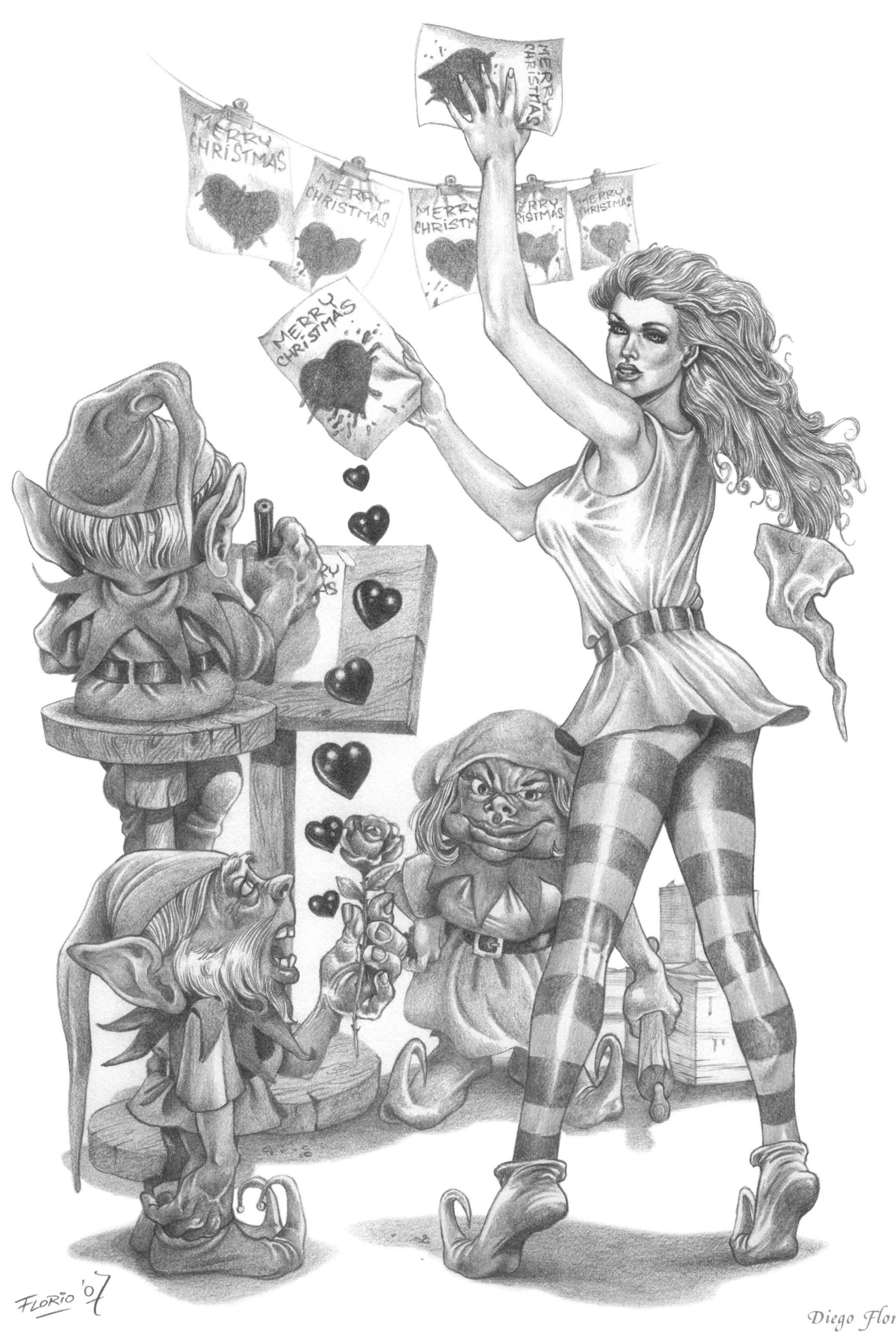

Diego Florio

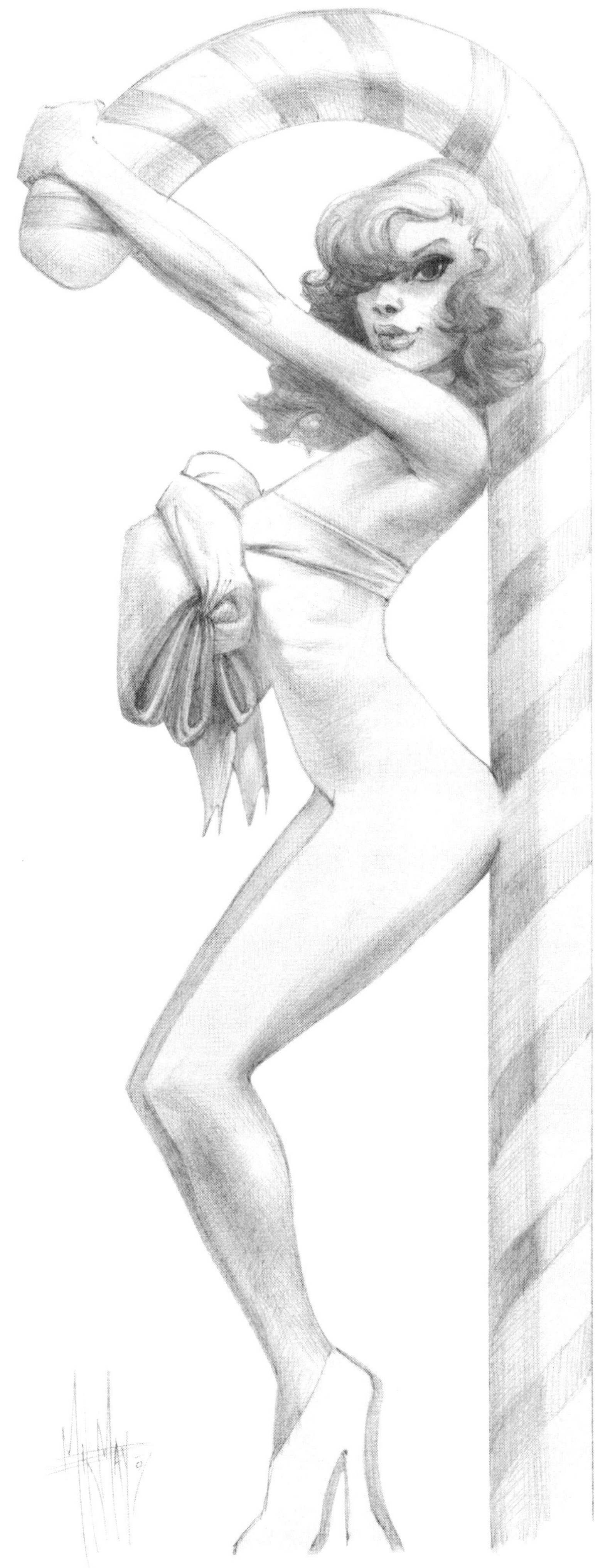

Mike May

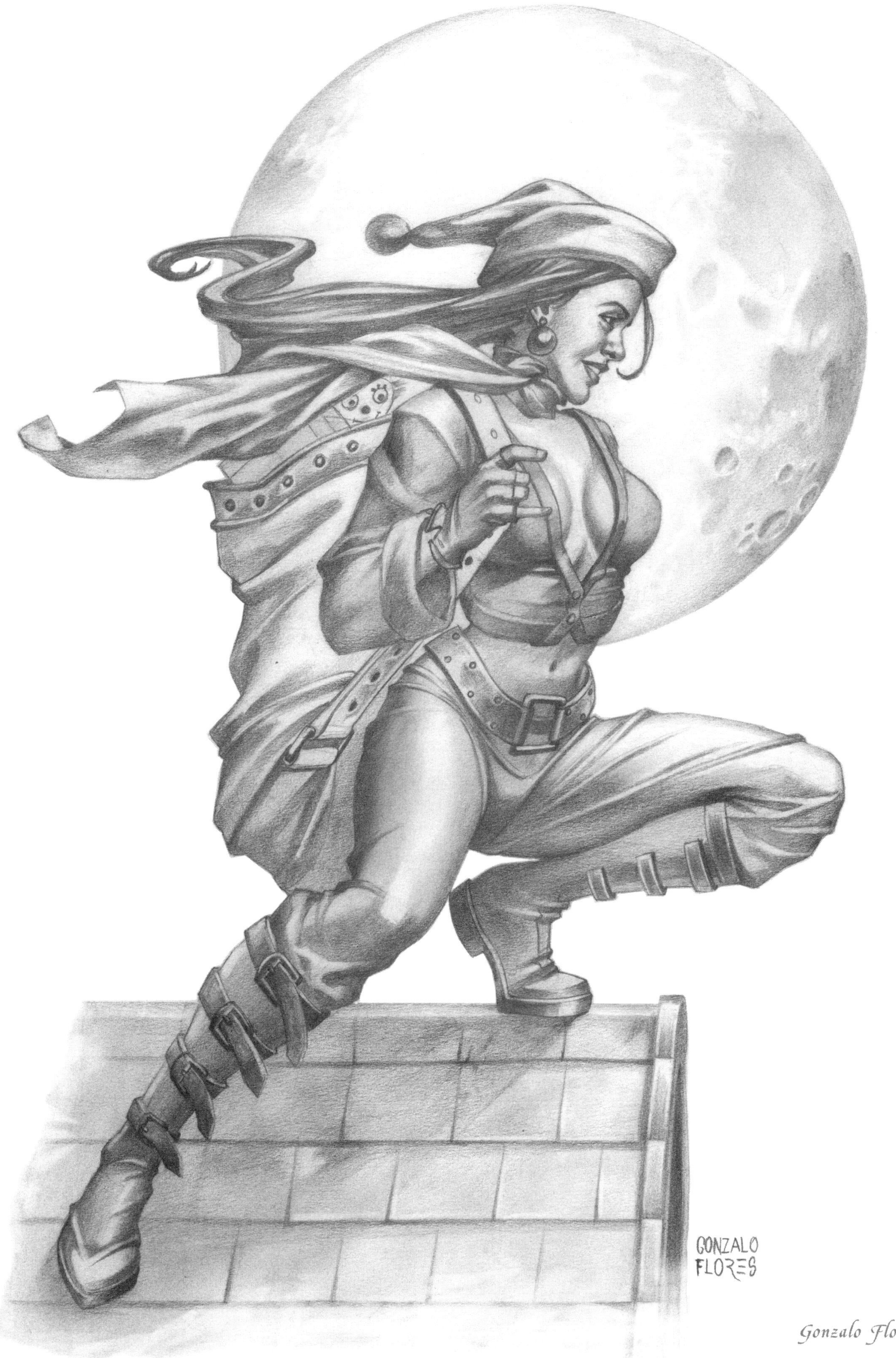

Gonzalo Flores

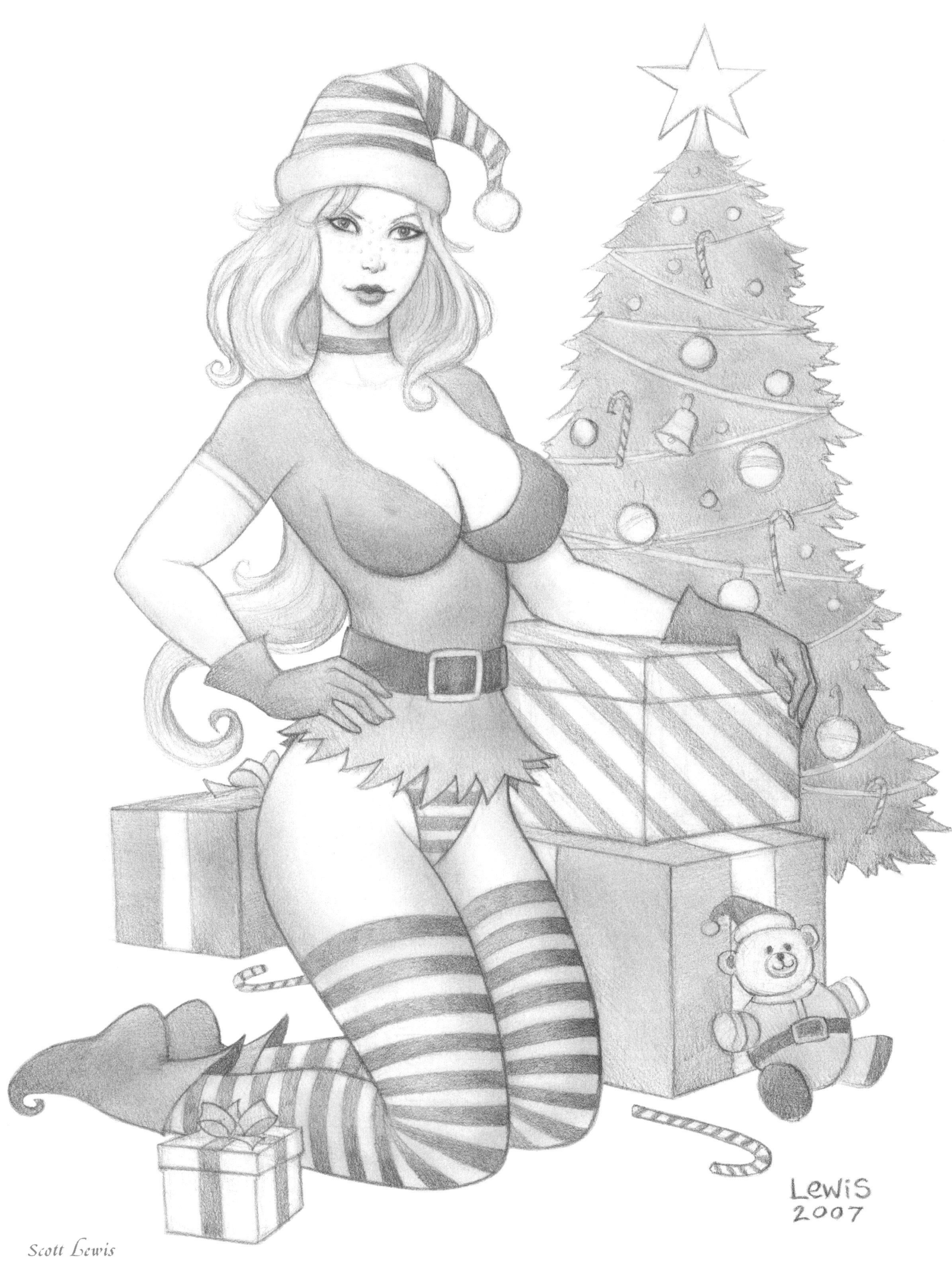

Scott Lewis

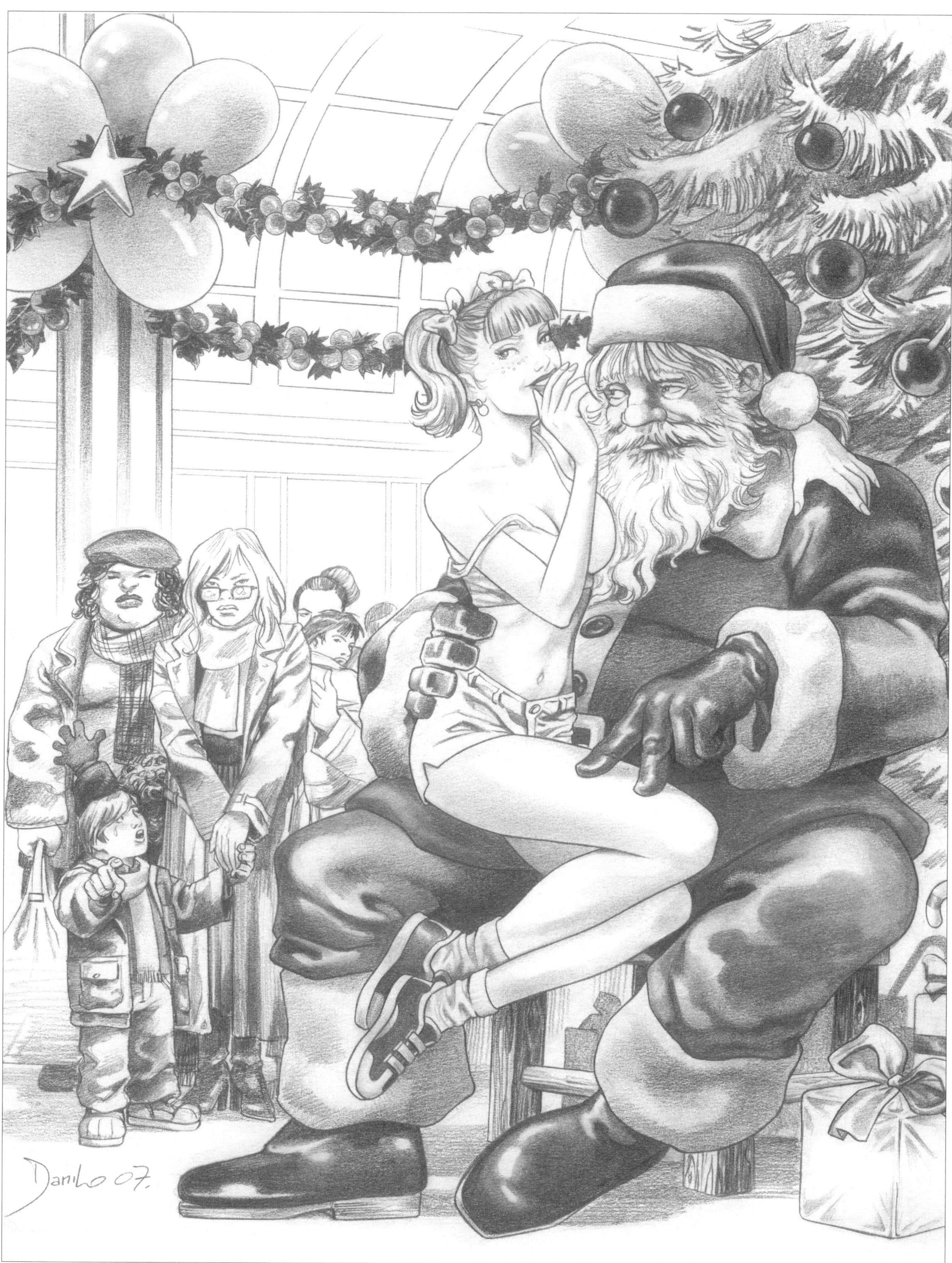

Danilo Guida

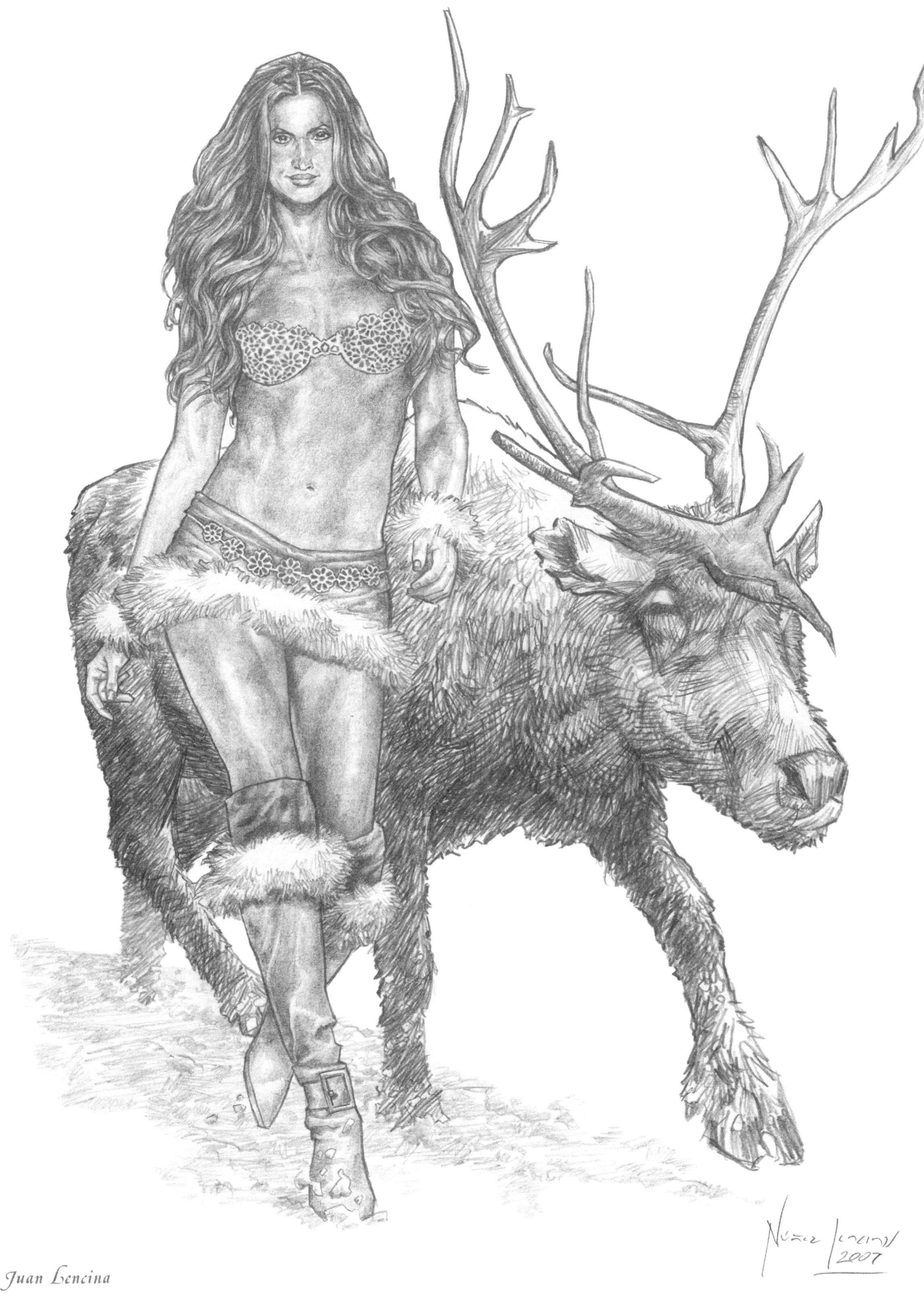

Juan Lencina

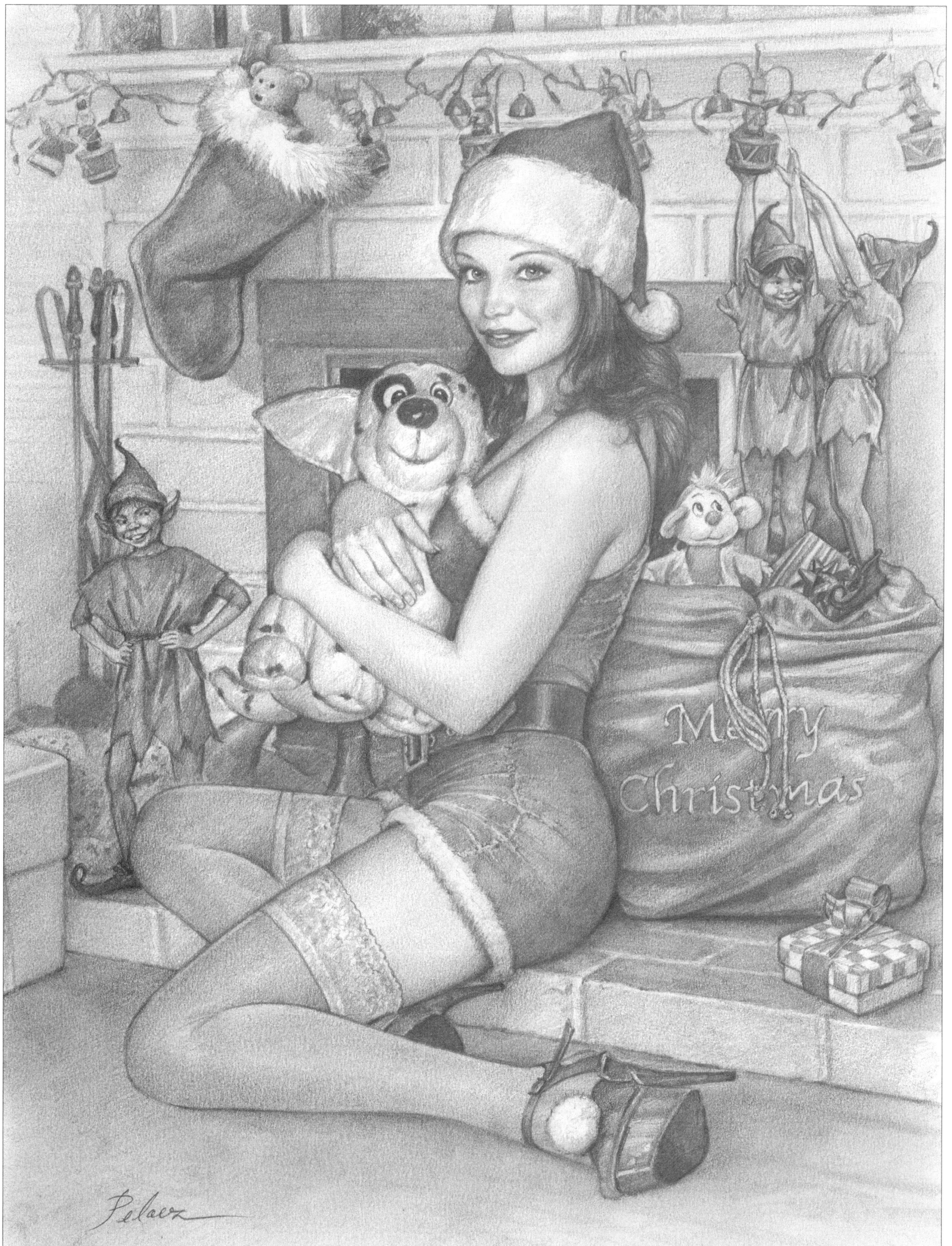

Pelaez

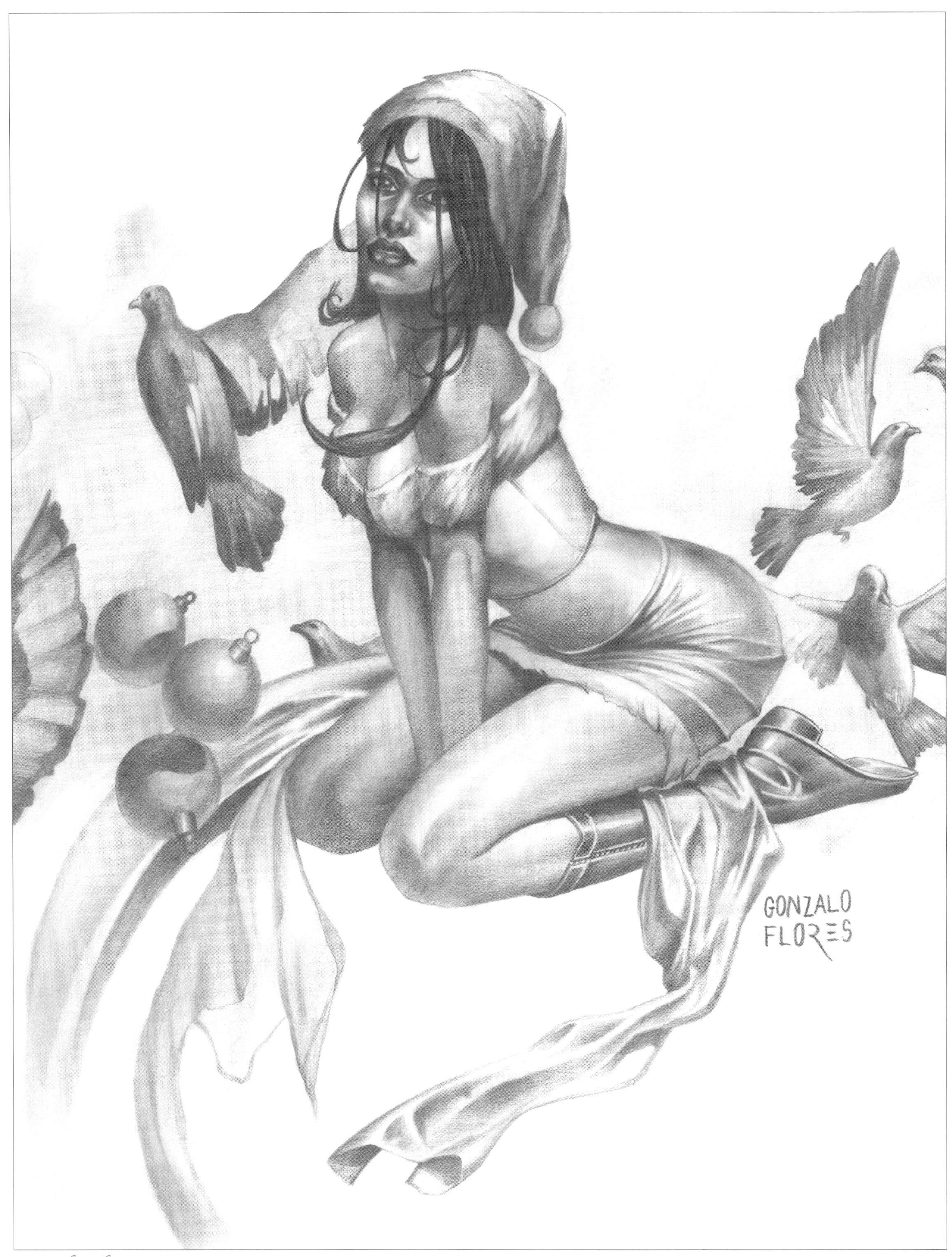

Gonzalo Flores

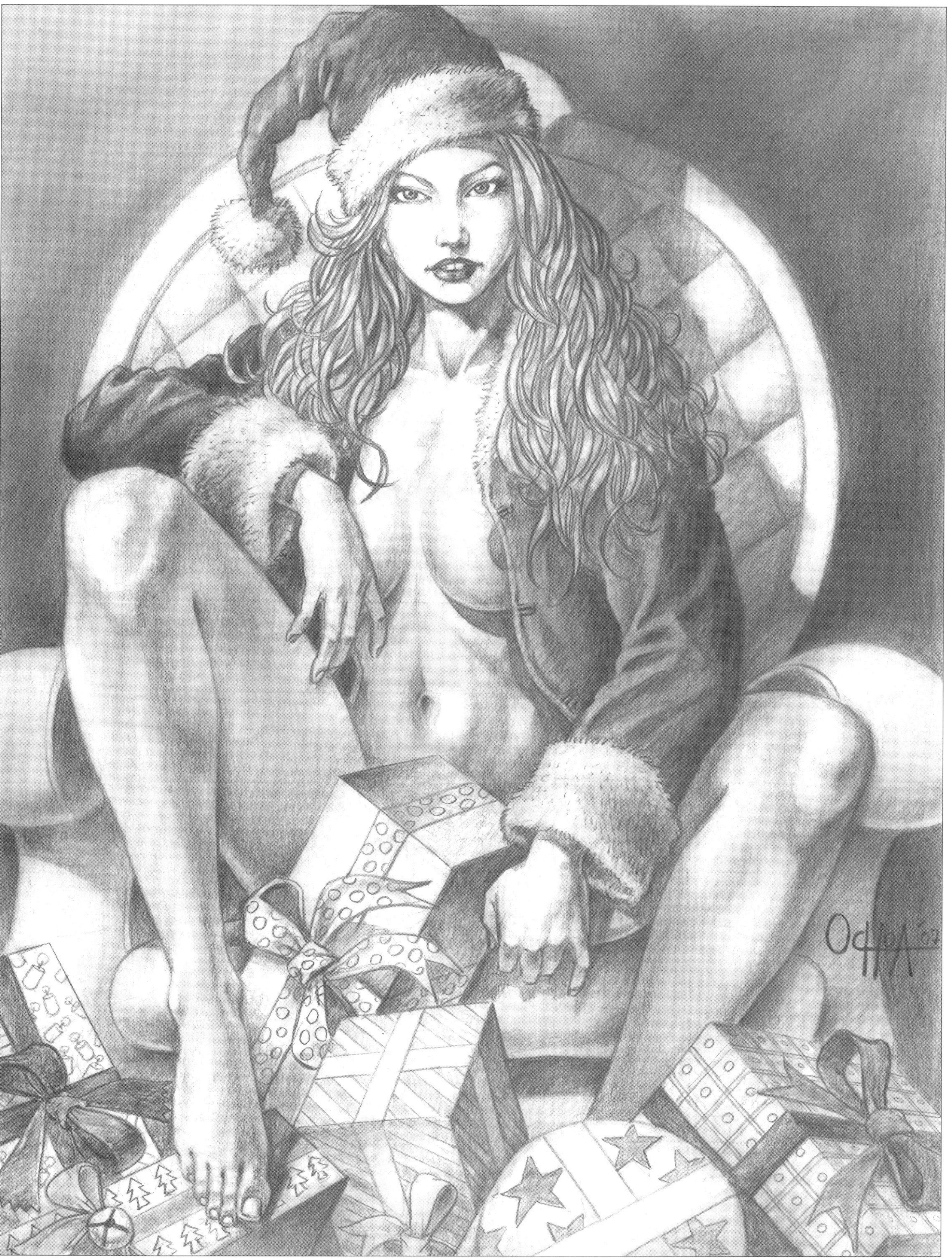

Percy Ochoa

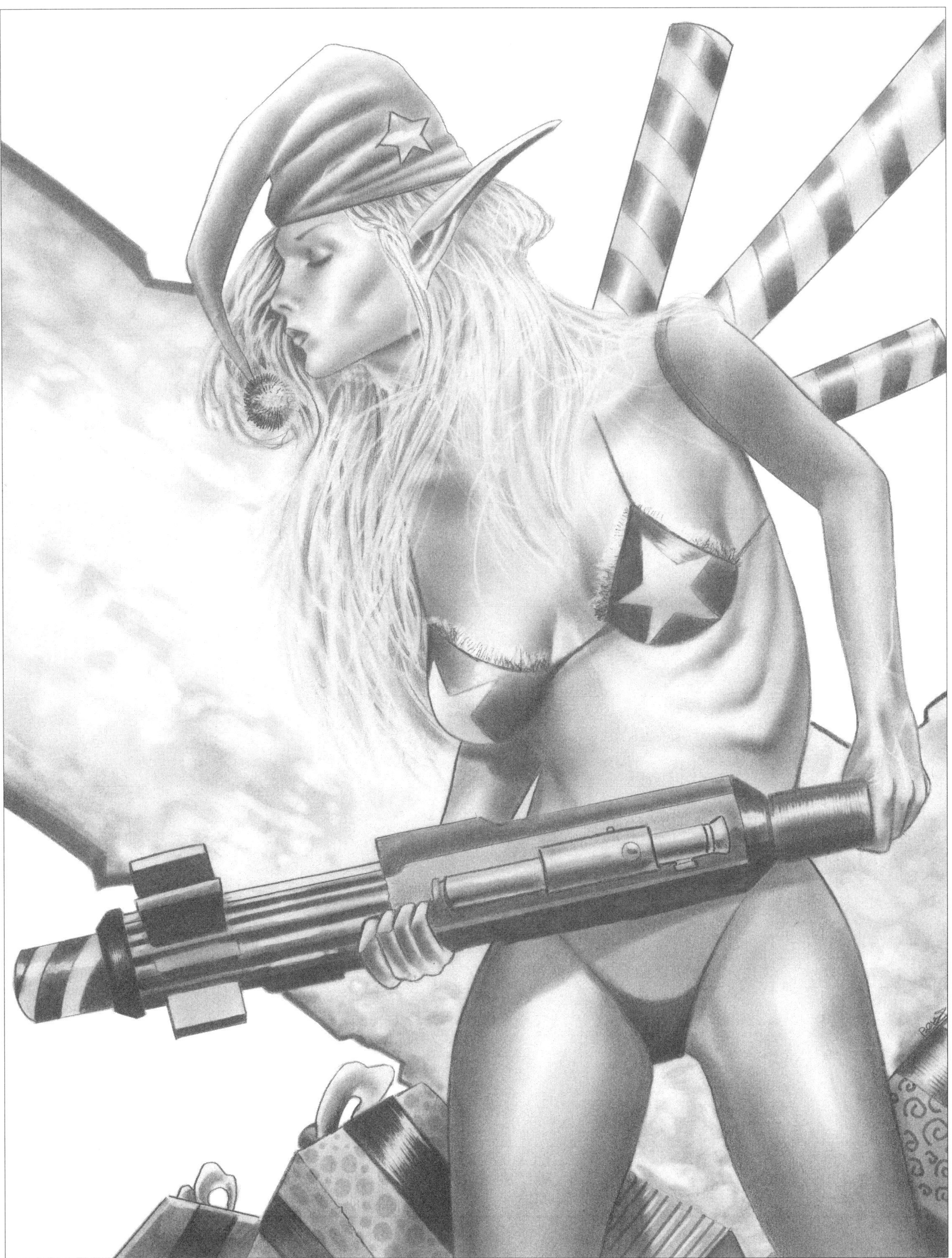

Luis Buci

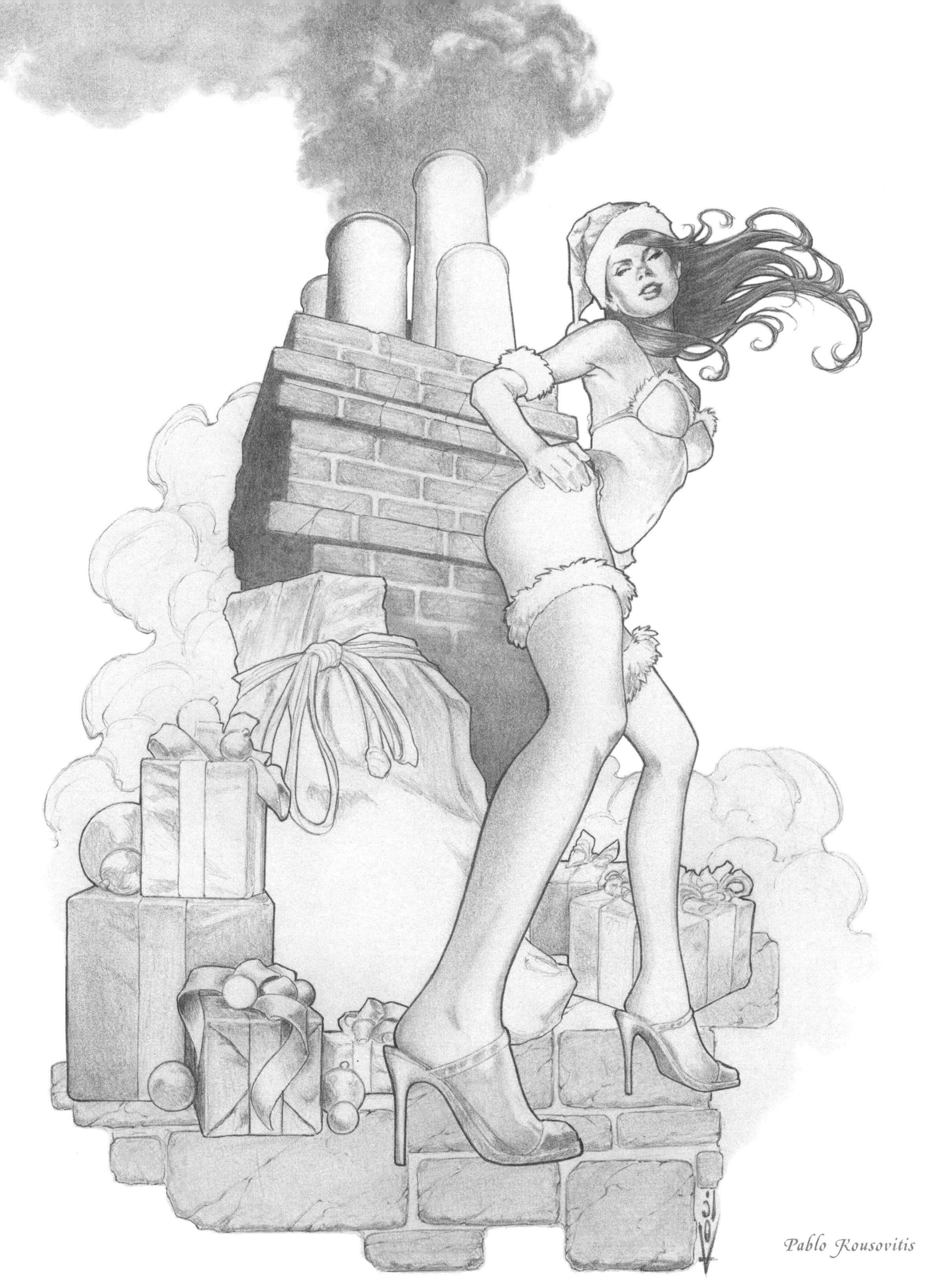

Pablo Kousovitis

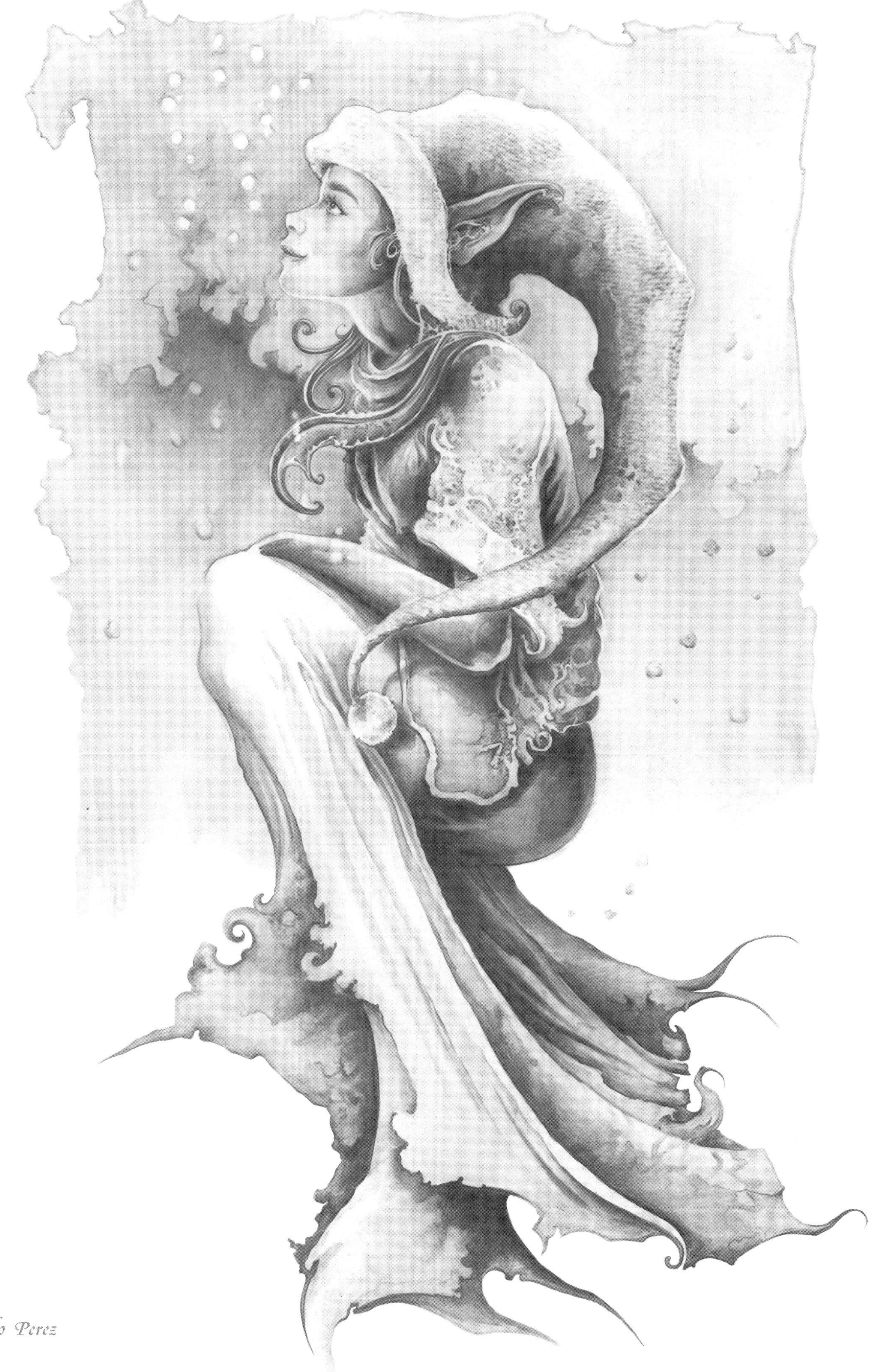

Aldo Perez

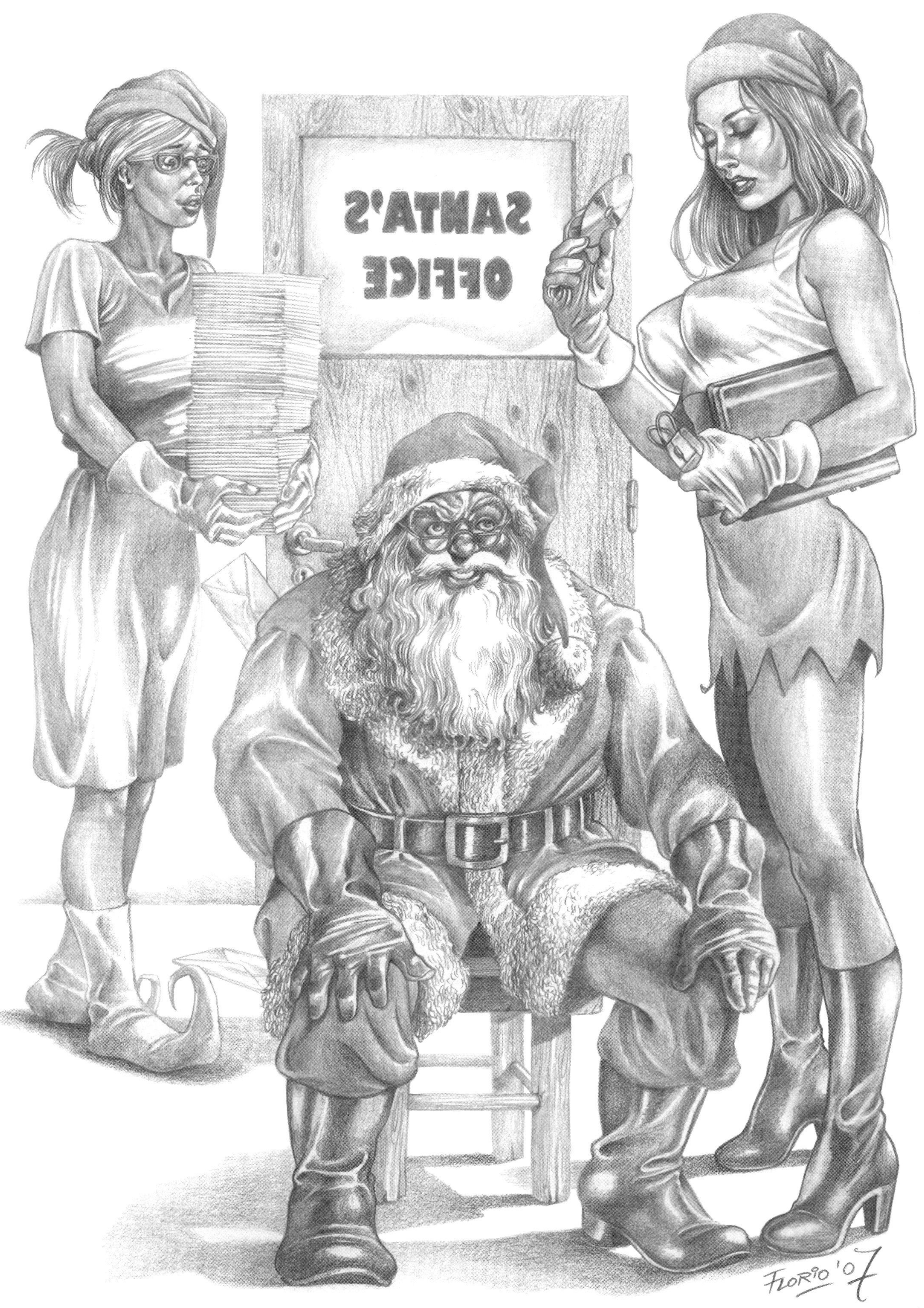

Diego Florio

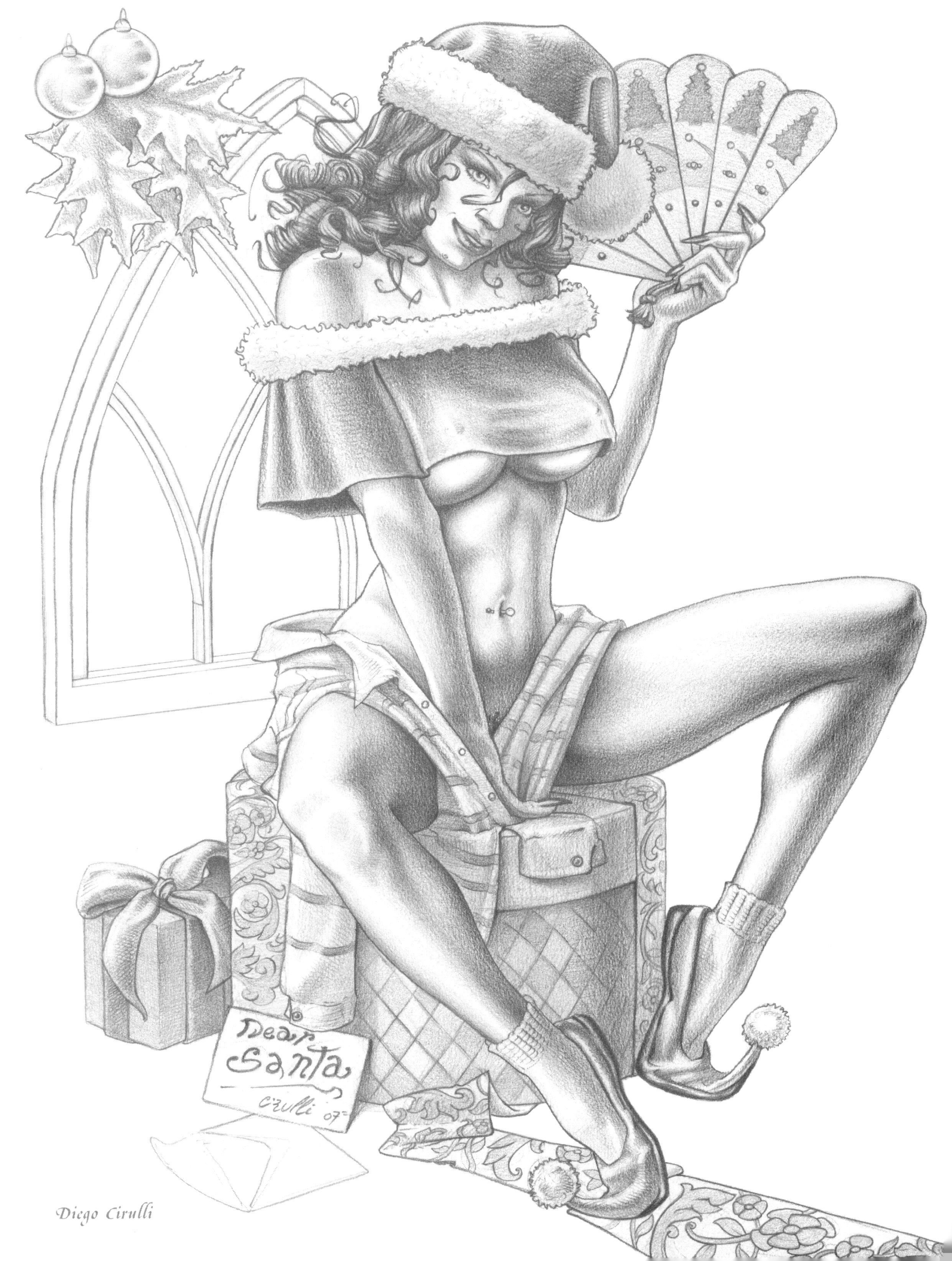

Diego Cirulli

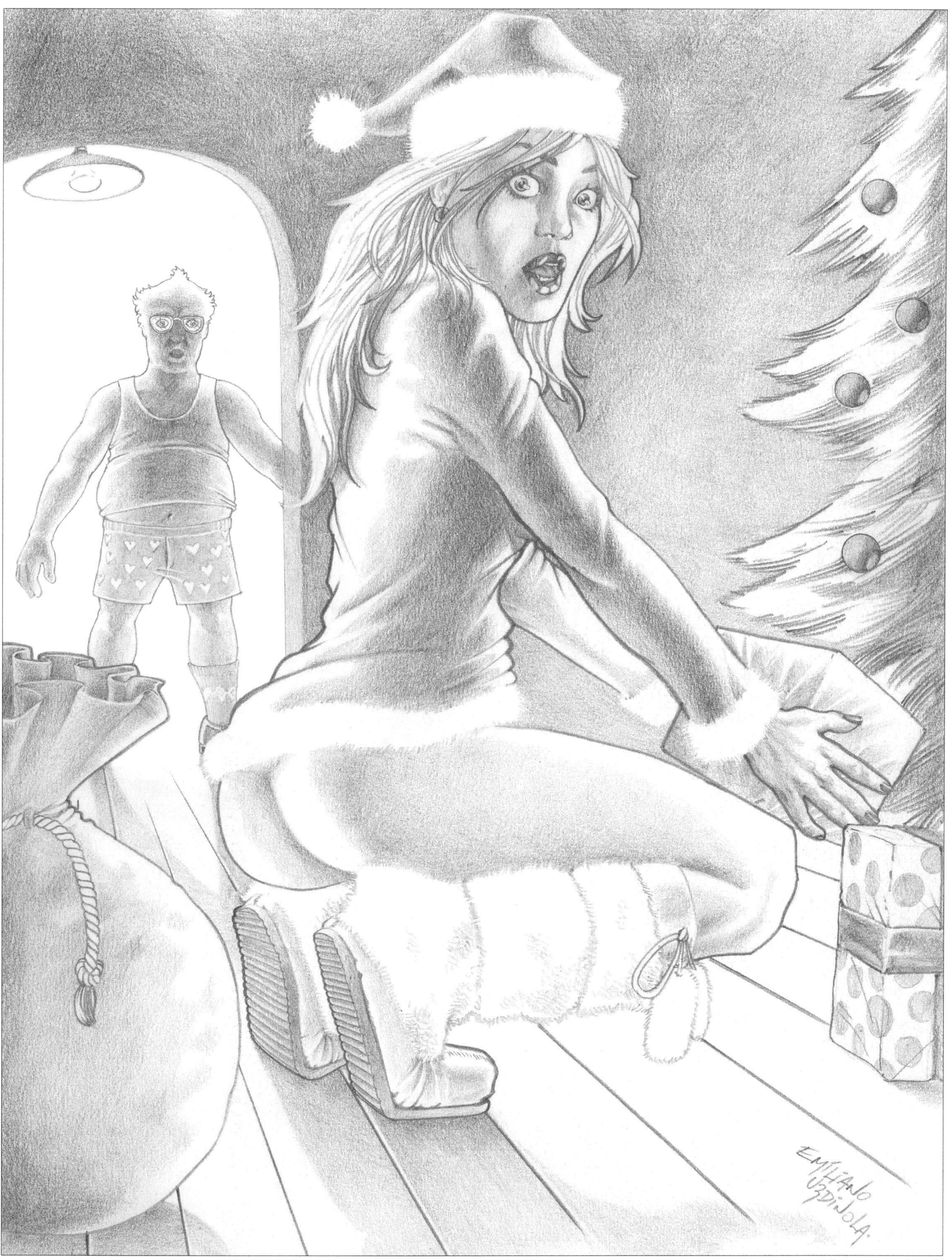

Emiliano Urdinola

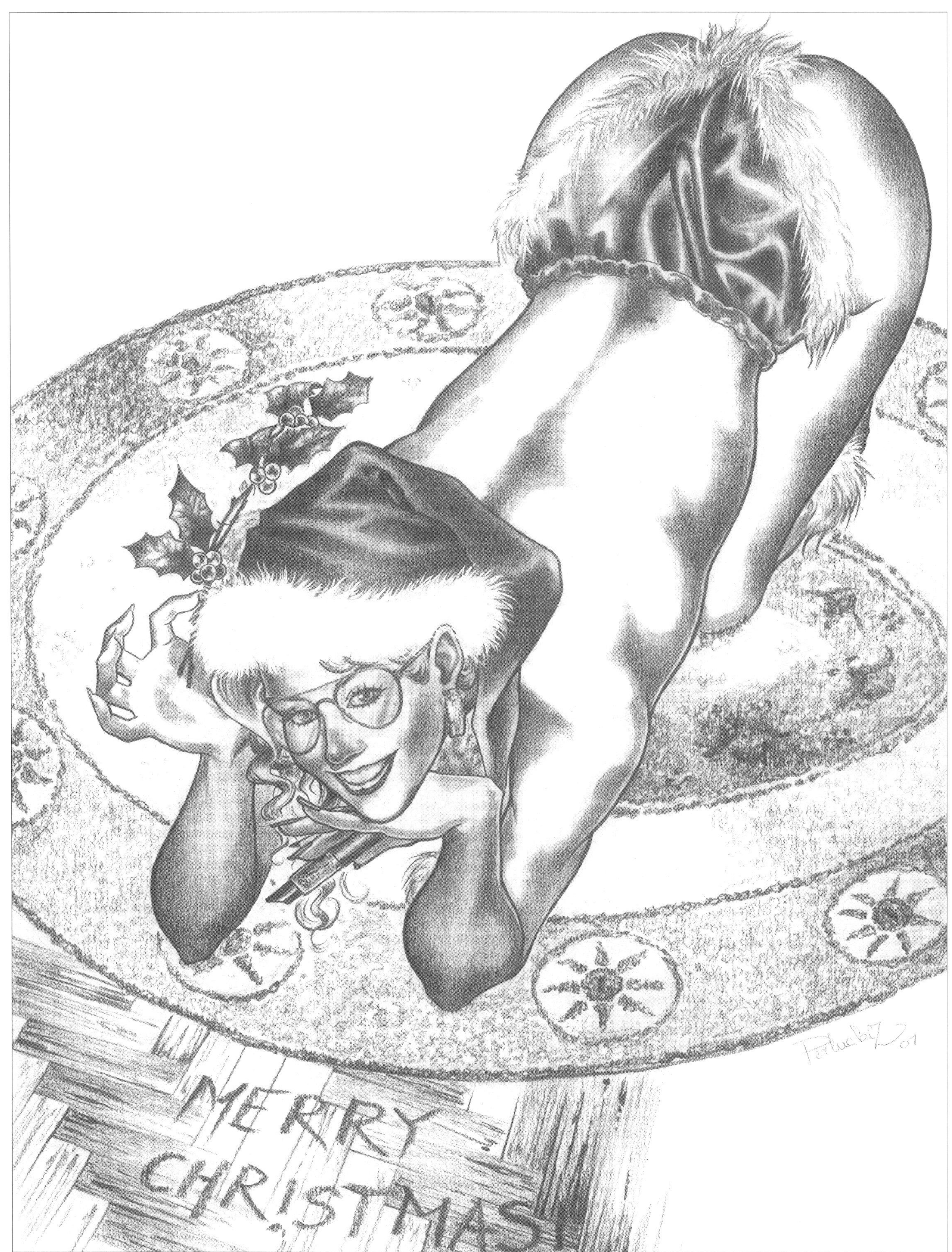

Perla Pilucki

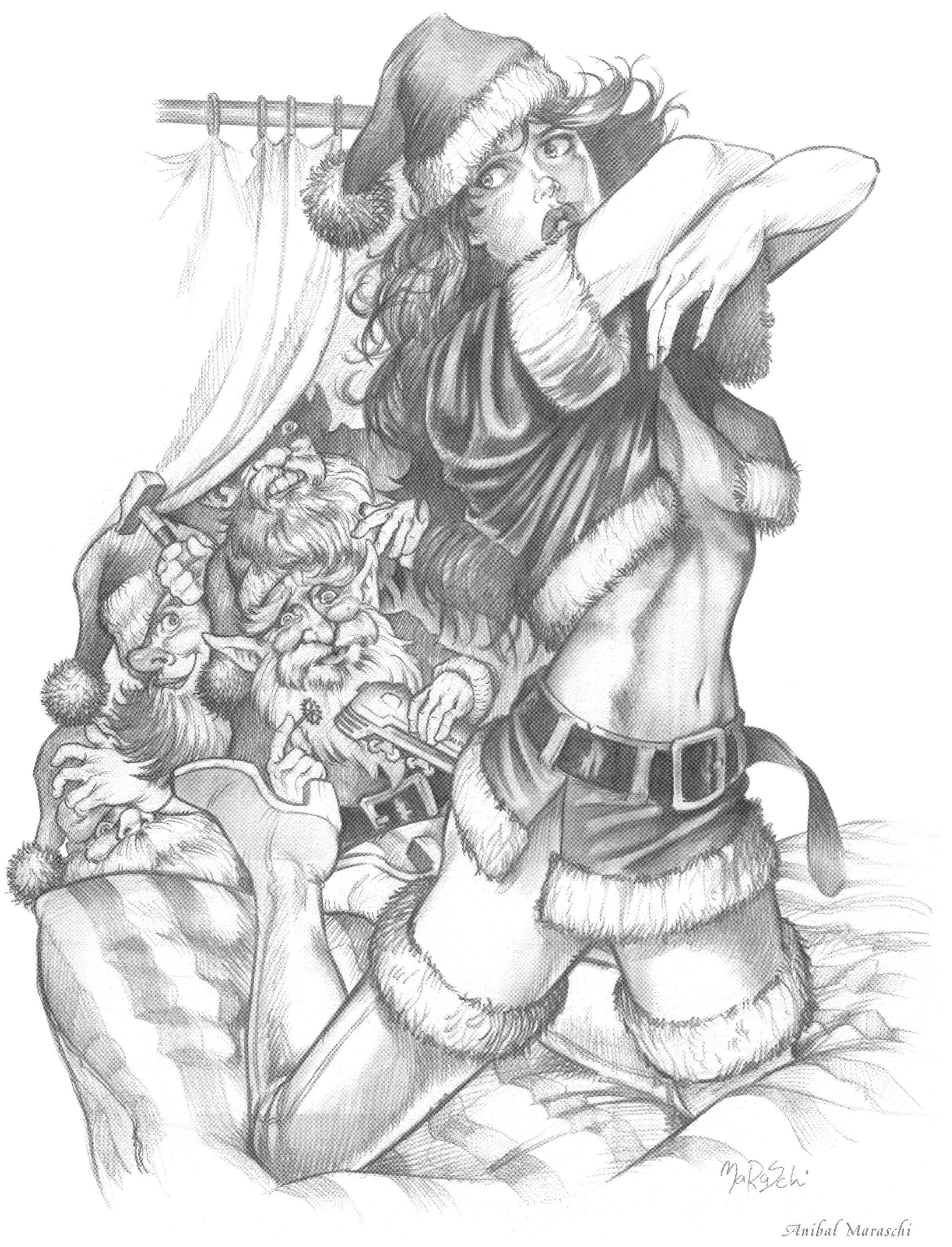

Anibal Maraschi

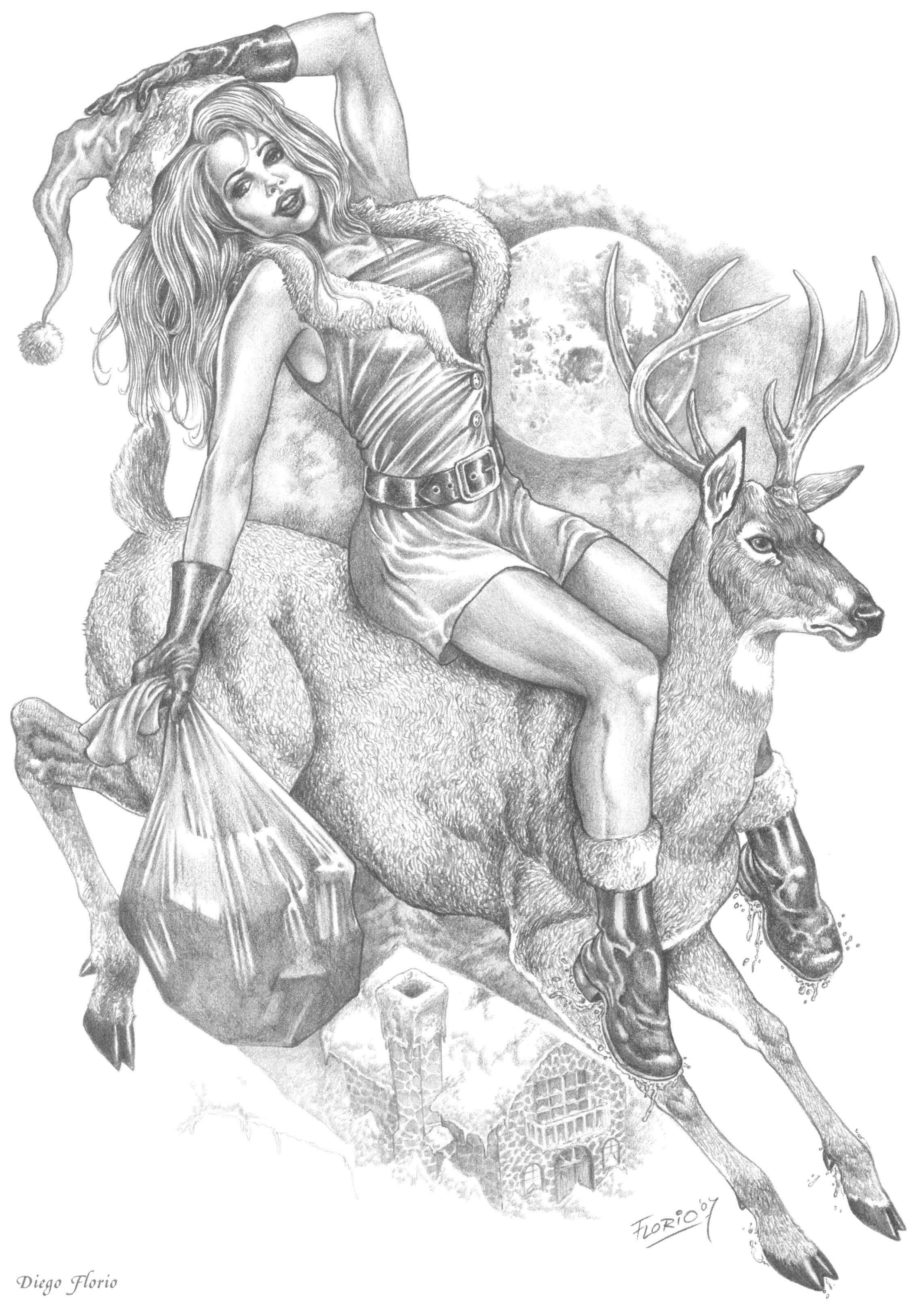

Diego Florio

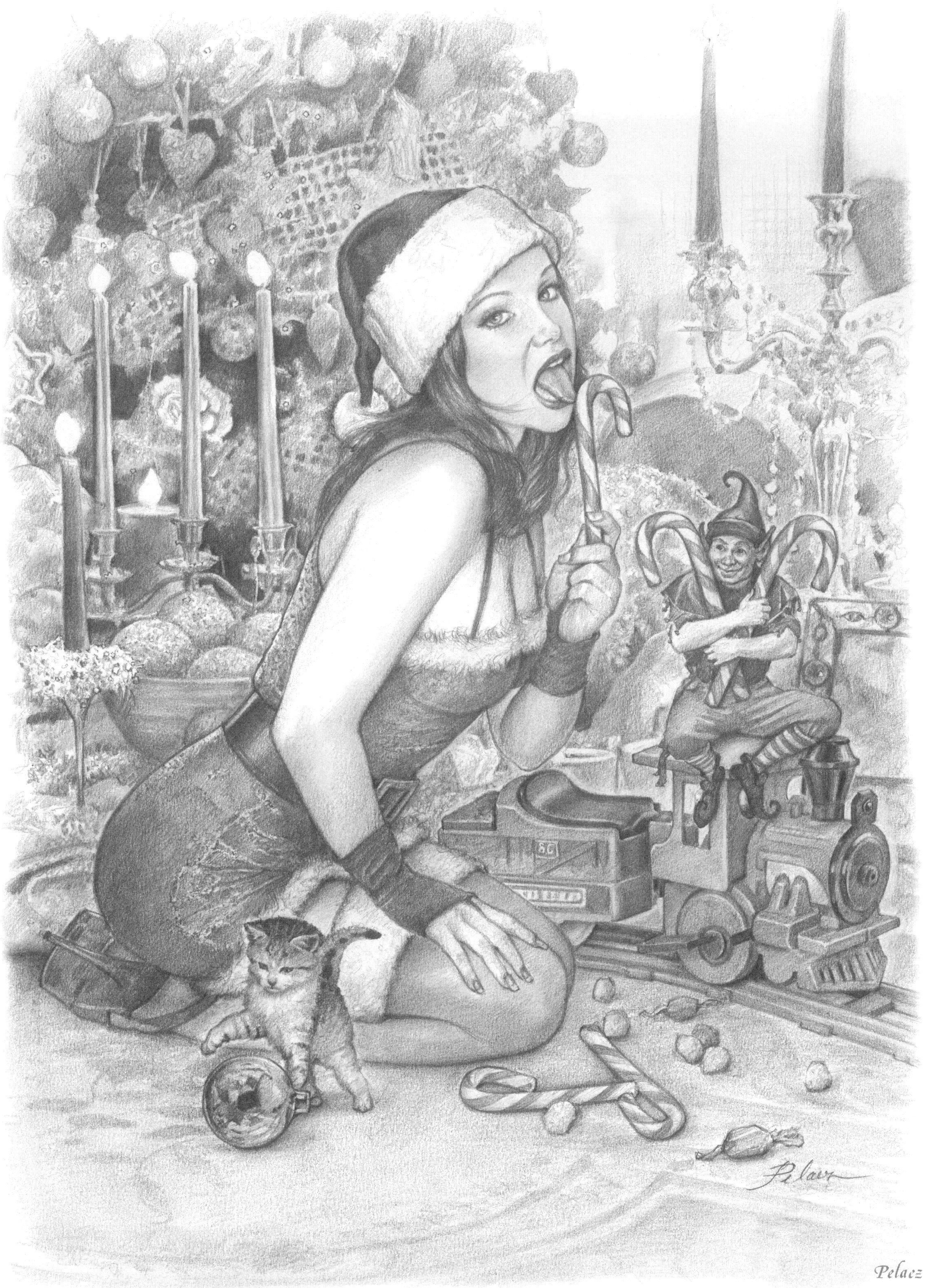

Pelaez

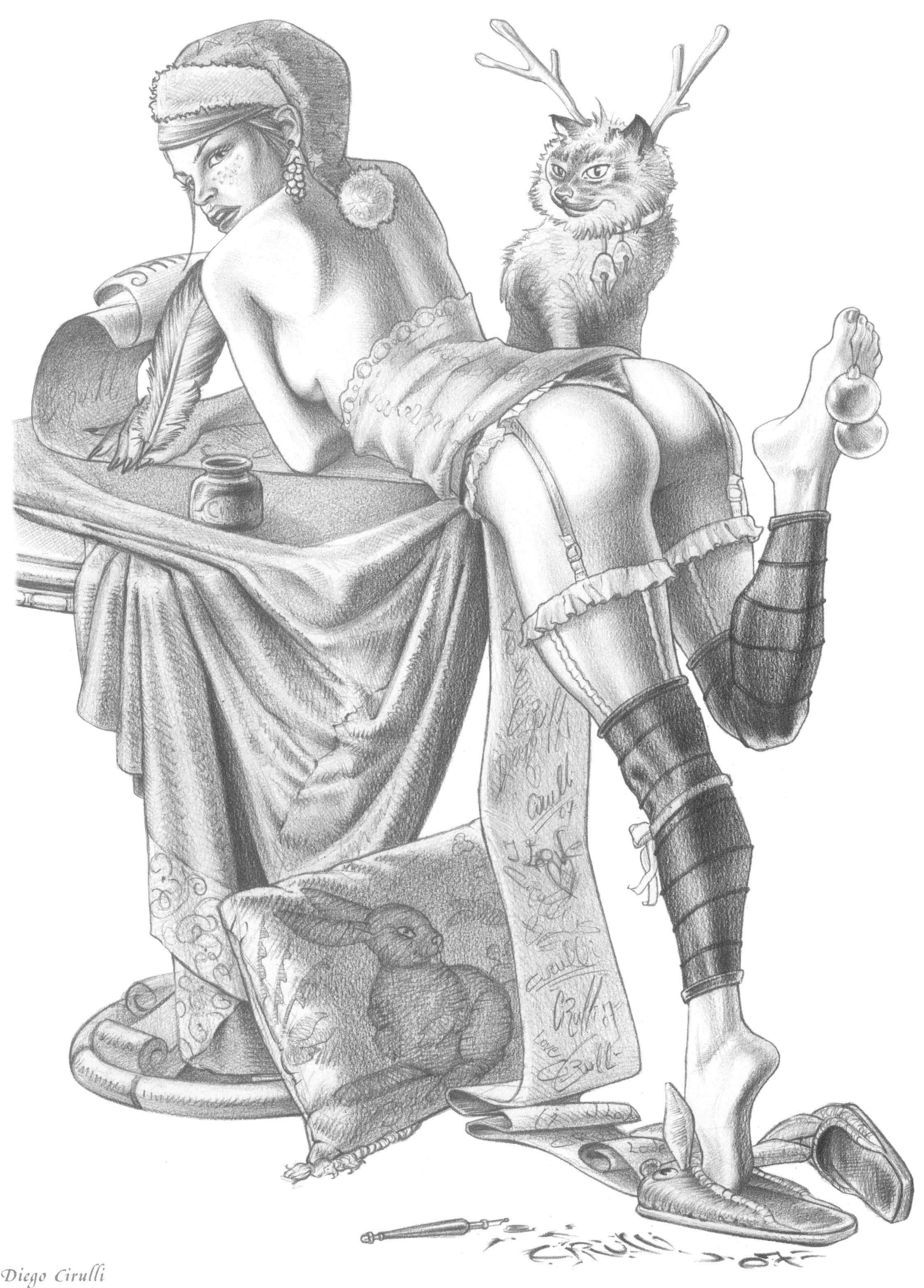

Diego Cirulli

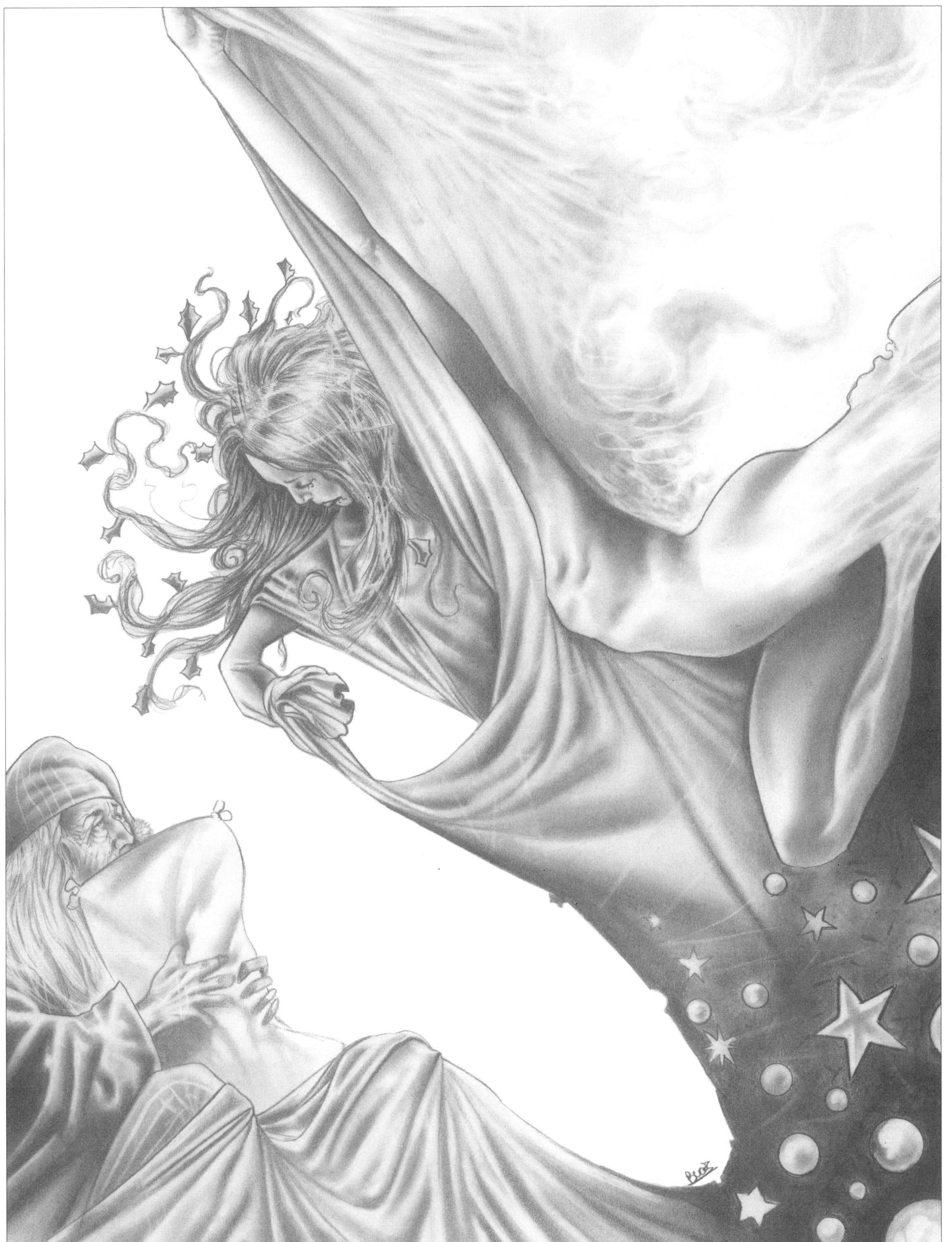

Luis Buci

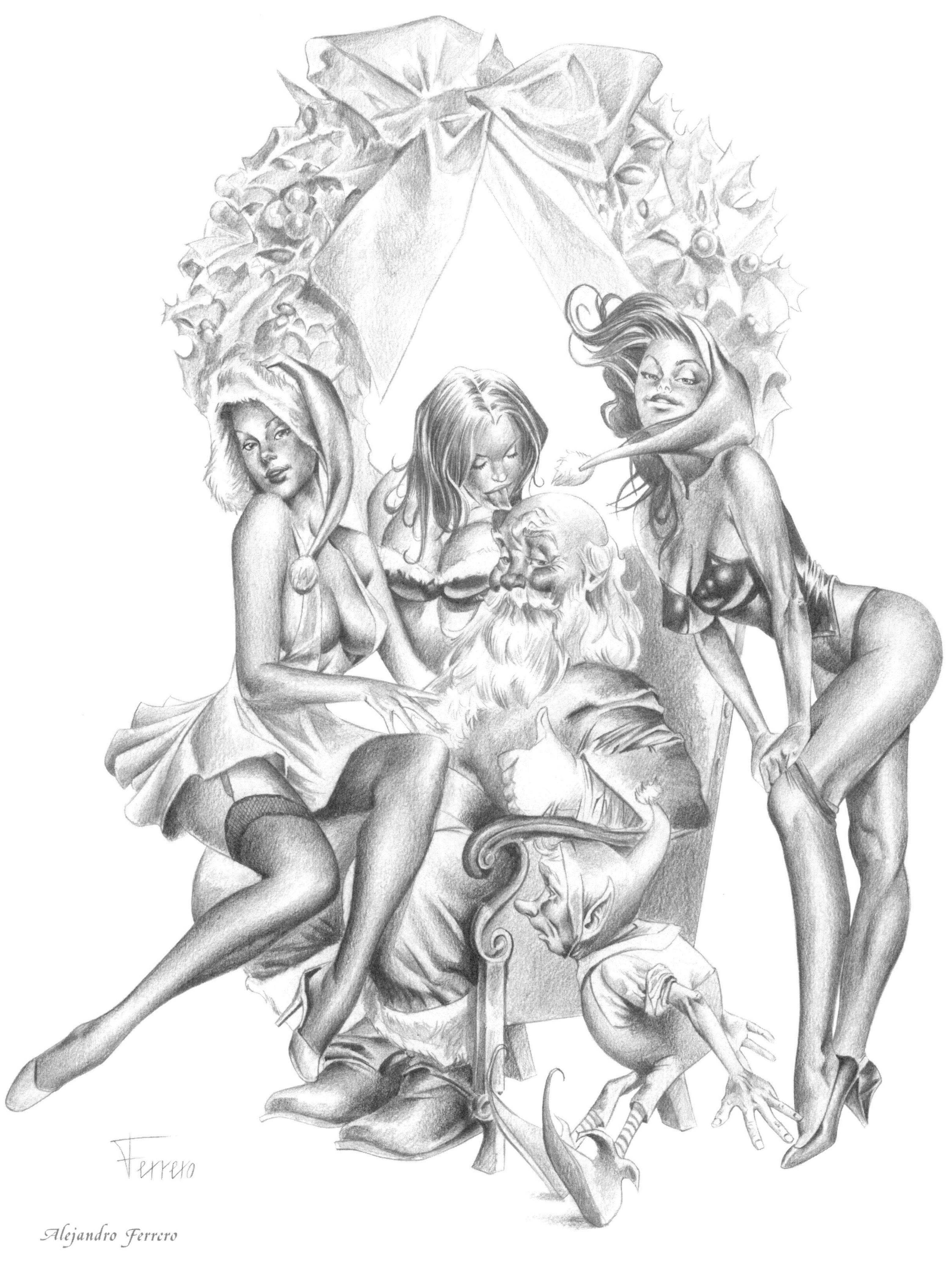

Alejandro Ferrero

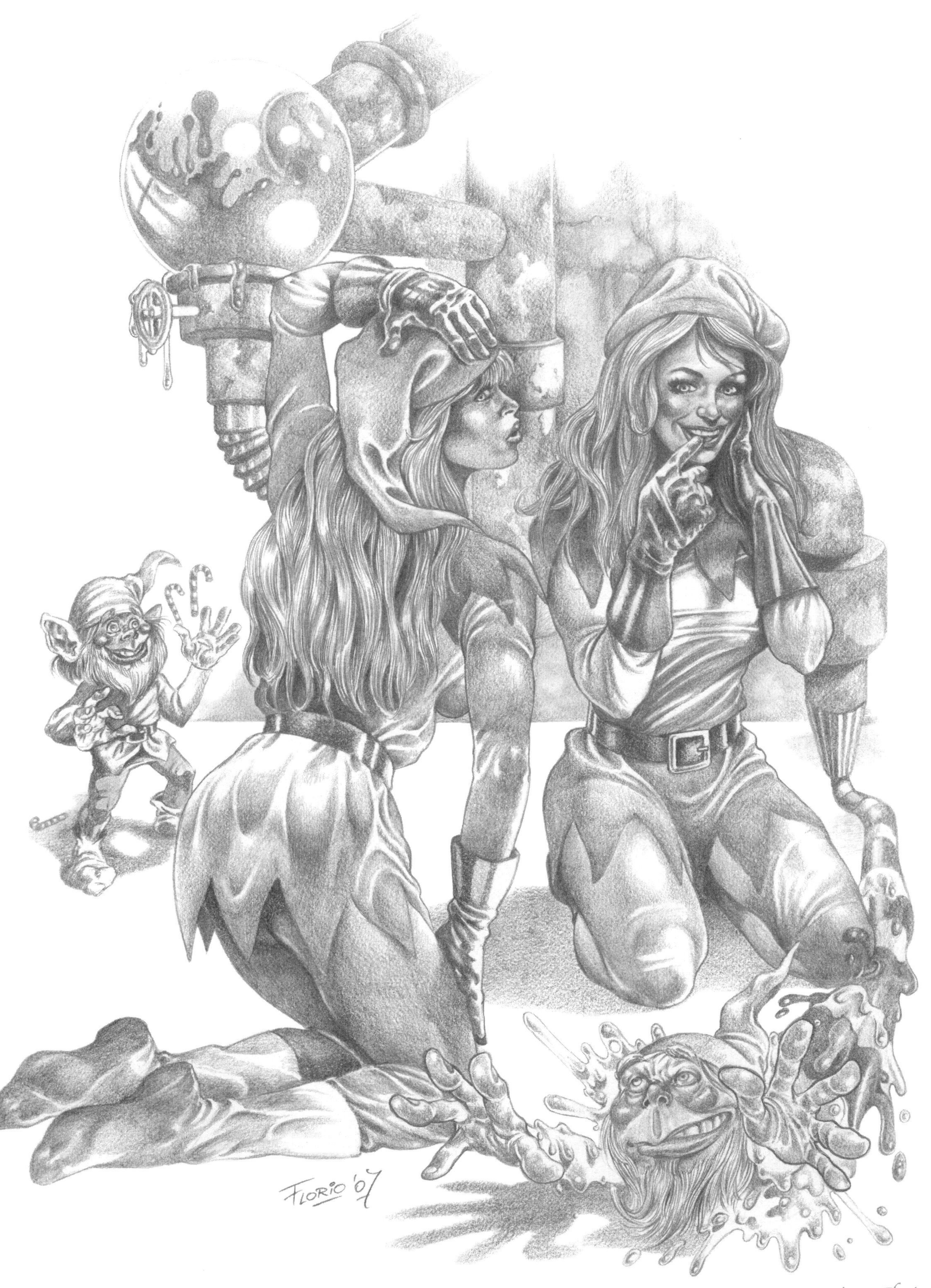

Diego Florio

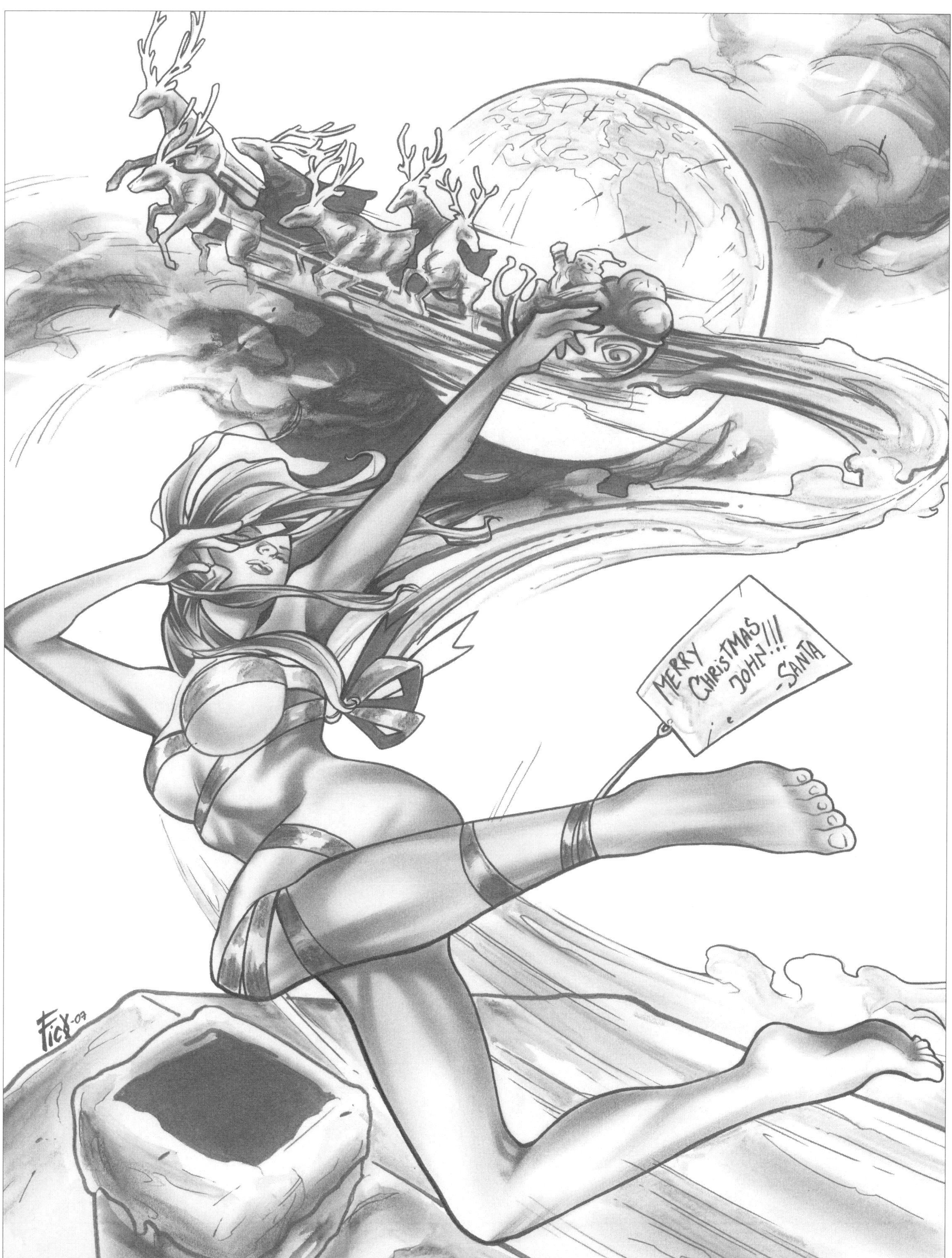

Federico Ossio

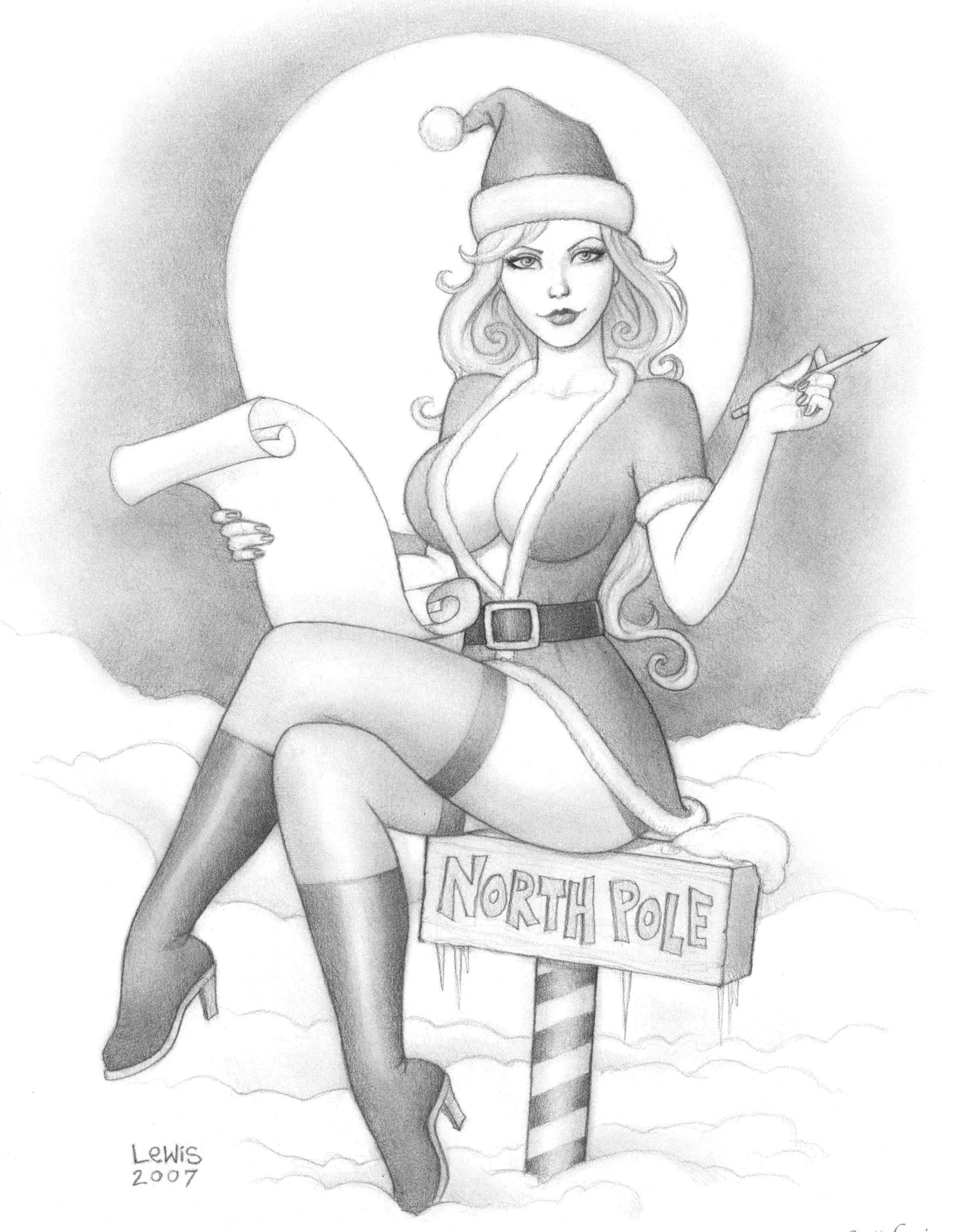

Scott Lewis

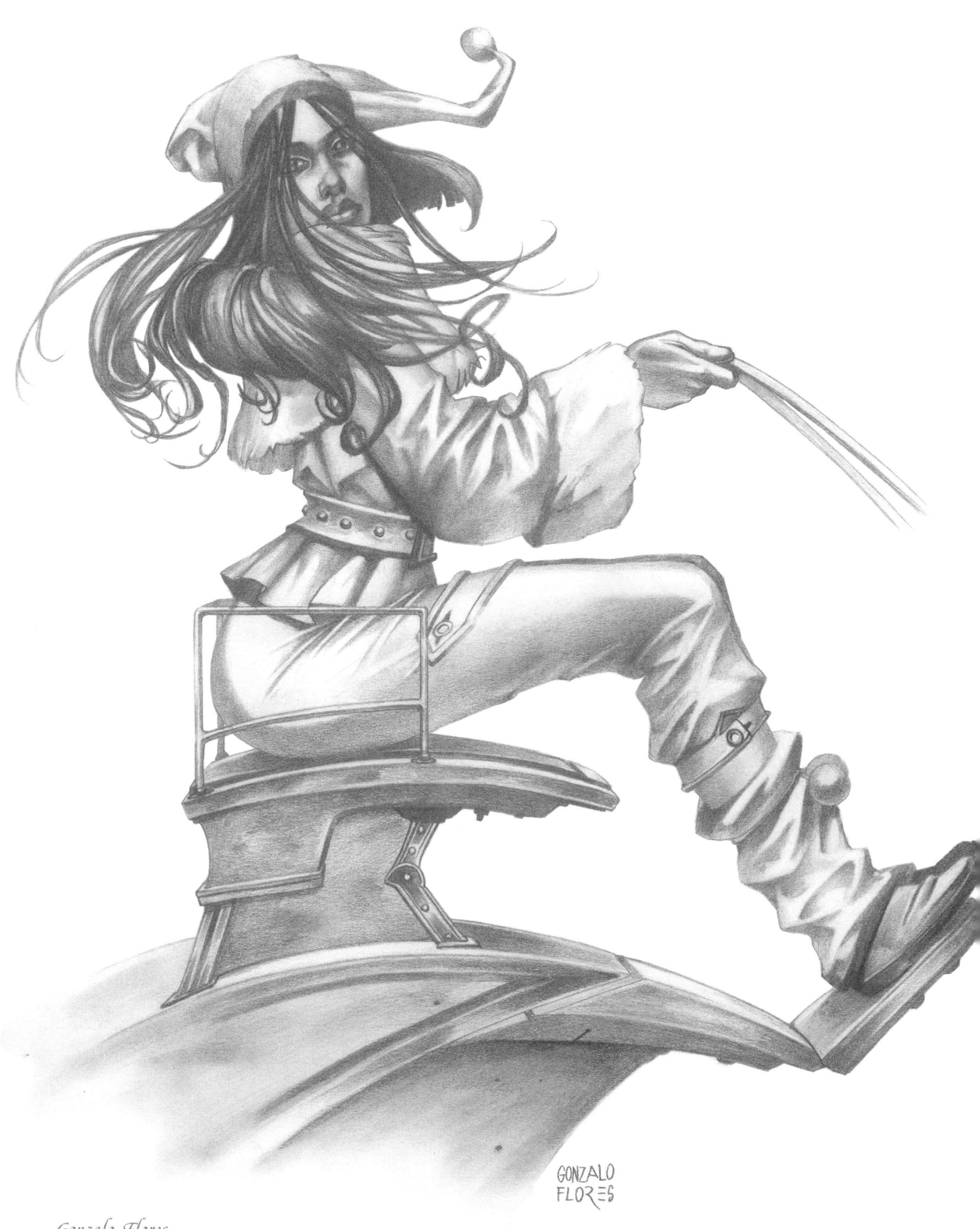

Gonzalo Flores

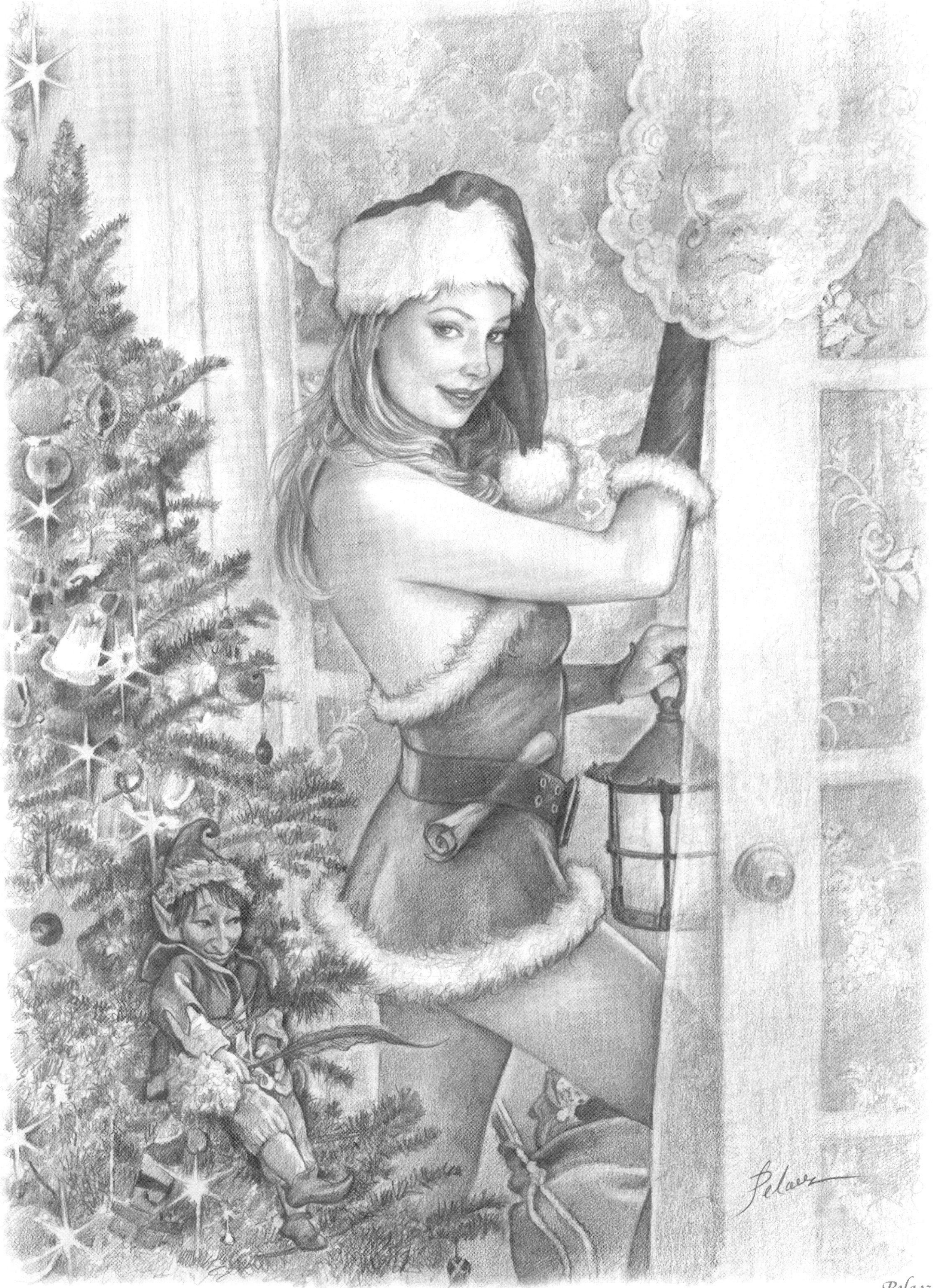

Pelaez

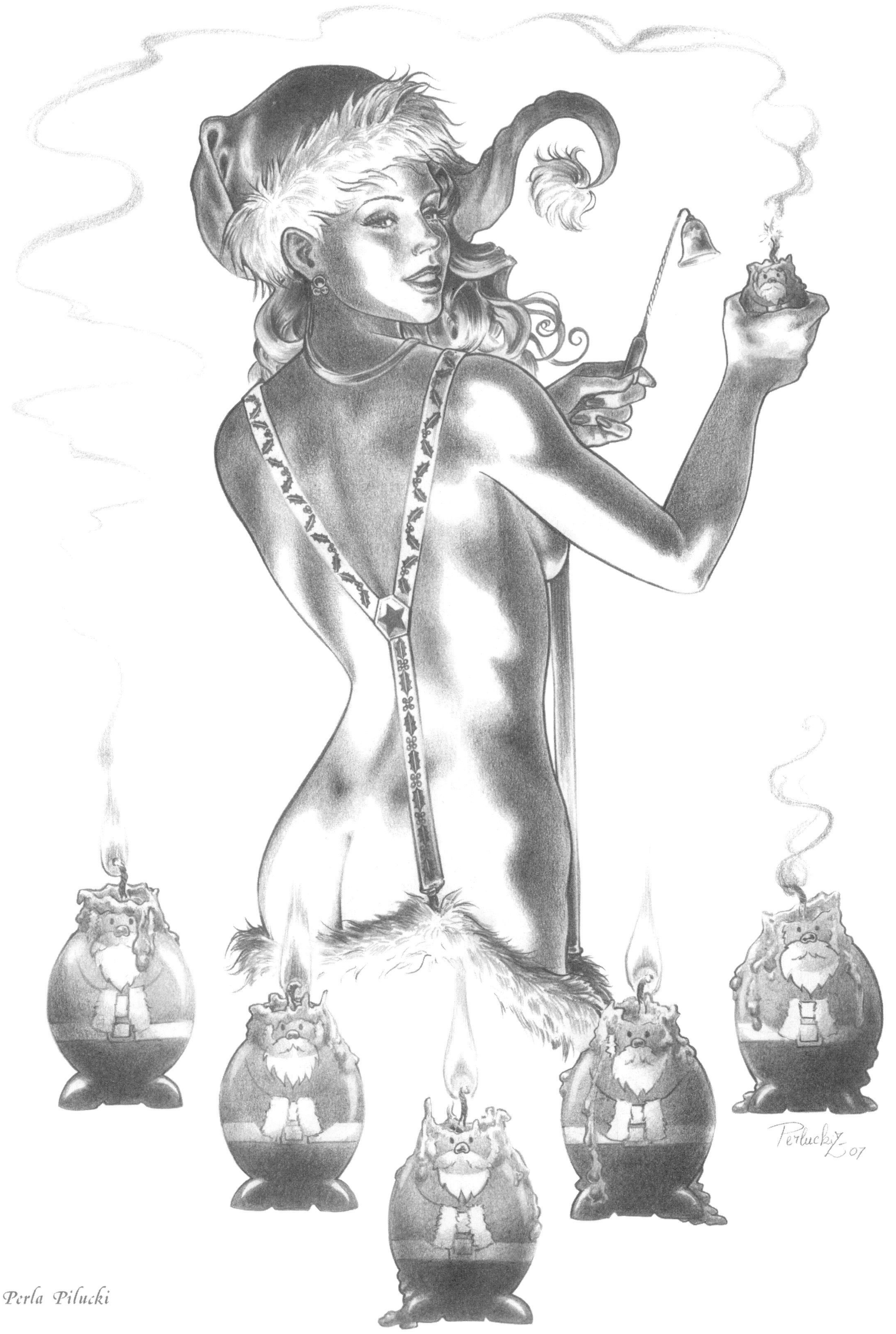

Perla Pilucki

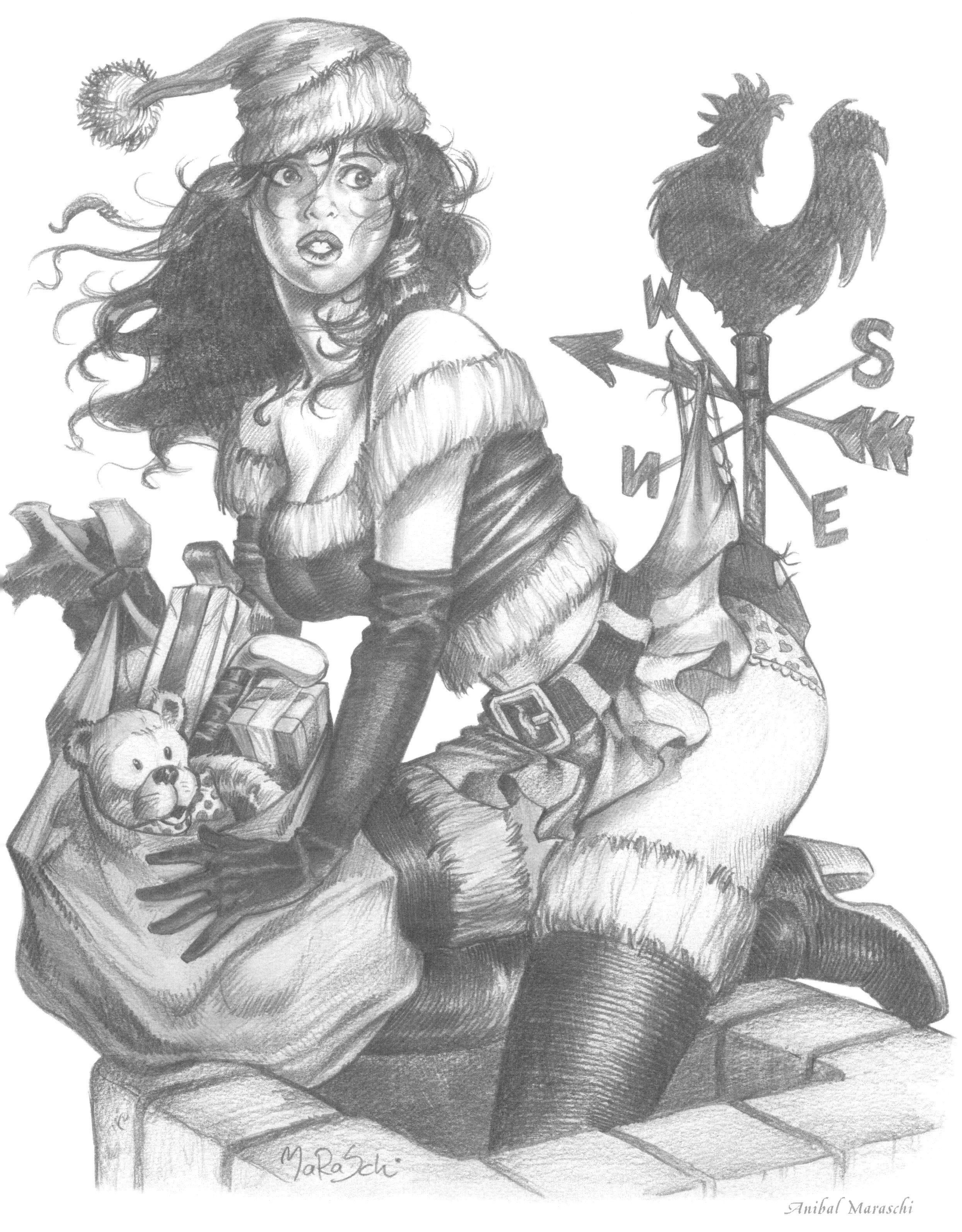

Anibal Maraschi

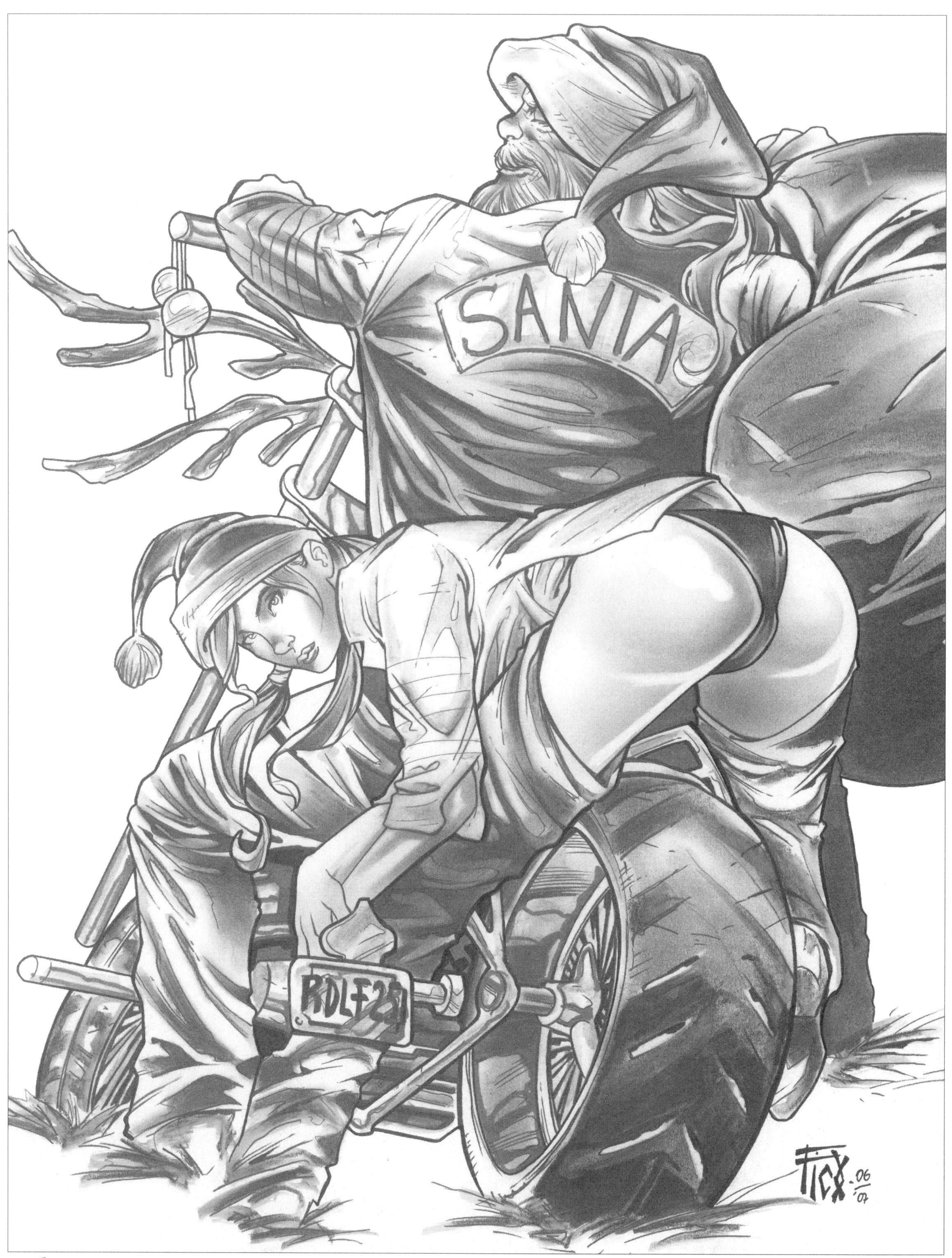

Federico Ossio